The Friendship Gap

Reaching Out across Cultures

Tim Stafford

InterVarsity Press
Downers Grove
Illinois 60515

To Popie

InterVarsity Press is the book-publishing division of Inter-Varsity Christian Fellowship, a student movement active on campus at hundreds of universities, colleges and schools of nursing. For information about local and regional activities, write IVCF, 233 Langdon St., Madison, WI 53703.

Distributed in Canada through InterVarsity Press, 860 Denison St., Unit 3, Markham, Ontario L3R 4H1, Canada.

All quotations of Scripture are taken from the Holy Bible: New International Version, *copyright* © *1978 by the New York International Bible Society. Used by permission of Zondervan Bible Publishers.*

Cover photograph: David Singer

ISBN 0-87784-975-7

Printed in the United States of America

Library of Congress Cataloging in Publication Data

Stafford, Tim.
    The friendship gap.

    Bibliography: p.
        1. Missionaries–Social conditions.   2. Missionaries–
Developing countries.   3. Cross-cultural studies.
4. Stafford, Tim.   I. Title.
HN32.S77   1984   303.4'82   84-6725
ISBN 0-87784-975-7

17	16	15	14	13	12	11	10	9	8	7	6	5	4	3	2	1
95	94	93	92	91	90	89	88	87	86	85	84					

Preface   9

1   The Snake & the Egg   *13*

2   Culture Fatigue   *29*

3   Bridging the Chasm of Culture   *41*

4   Those Rich Foreigners   *57*

5   At Home with the Language   *79*

6   When Values Clash   *93*

7   Colonialism: A Persistent Complaint   *111*

8   Who's in a Hurry?   *125*

9   True Sacrifice—and Not-Quite-True   *135*

Notes   *145*

Acknowledgments

As a guard against my own eccentricities of thought and experience, I have asked a number of missionaries and other Christians from around the world to read and criticize the manuscript of this book. Their comments and additions have been invaluable, and I would like to thank them, though listing names is hardly adequate recognition for what they have contributed. They are Joseph Aryee, the Rev. Seth Aryee, Sam Atiemo, Randy and Carrie Bare, Paul and Mary Jeanne Buttrey, Emi Gichinga, Norma Kelly, Bedan Mbugua, G. Hunter and Edith Norwood, Peter and Jan Payne, Joyce Scott, Gary and Marlene Van Brocklin, Haron Wachira and Philip Yancey. Nearly all of these are close friends who have also contributed to my thinking through letters and conversation. Philip Yancey's contribution goes far beyond that, for he has been the shadow behind nearly all my writing since I left college, and I owe him more than I can say for his friendship and his skill.

I am not sure which of the ideas in this book are originally mine and which my wife Popie's. She is a sharp observer of human beings, delighting in their oddities. We have experienced great joy talking through what I share here. She has been both encourager and critic—a difficult combination. In thanks for our good years together, and in hopes of many more, I dedicate this book to her.

Preface

This book comes from my four-year experience in Kenya as a missionary. I make no claim to the broad study required for genuine expertise, and this book is not by any means an academic treatise. It is a purely personal reflection.

I see my danger. Few things are so irritating as the self-proclaimed expert, ready to explain and solve all the problems of, say, India, after a stay of a few weeks or years. If and when such arrogance creeps into my words, I hope those who know better will kindly overlook it. I mean no harm.

I hope for something different, and less, than expertise. I aim to help other novices. Sometimes a beginner can explain things better than a veteran can, for the novice remembers how things look from the newcomer's angle. As C. S. Lewis wrote, "The fellow-pupil can help more than the master because he knows less. The difficulty we want him to explain is one he has recently met. The expert met it so long ago that he has forgotten. He sees the whole subject, by now, in such a different light that he cannot conceive what is really troubling the pupil."[1]

New missionaries find themselves thrown into an utterly strange cultural setting, confronted with choices they are little prepared for. To older, experienced missionaries this strangeness no longer stands out with dramatic clarity. They have adapted to it and have become concerned rather with questions of strategy and organization. They remember their early struggles as a bygone victory, like a big exam in high school, or their first date. It no longer seems dangerous. The more expert they become, the broader their view and the less vividly they may remember the particular struggles. The experienced person is like a man high up on the cliffs, watching someone struggle through thick underbrush in the valley below, calling encouragement to him. Such a higher view is absolutely necessary. But it may be of less immediate succor than the words of the man three paces ahead, who slammed through the same tangle moments before.

So, at least, I hope. The memory of my struggles is fresh.

This book is for *new* missionaries. Most of the material deals with the typical missionary situation: someone from a Western country going to a Third World country. Other missionaries—such as those to Europe, or from Korea, or from one culture to another within America—should find the material helpful, but they will have to adapt it to their own situations. A missionary from Ghana to Kenya, for instance, pointed out to me that his problems with the barrier of money are different from those I describe.

What do I mean by "missionary"? Several definitions can be used, but the one I prefer is this: a missionary is someone whose main work is building the church of Jesus Christ in another culture. Thus, a missionary may be a white suburbanite working as an evangelist on the South Side of Chicago, or a black New Yorker working as a Bible teacher in Iowa. A missionary's job may be fixing airplane engines, or making high-caliber audio cassettes, but he does it to help establish the church in another culture.

The Western church in this century has kept a reasonably

consistent flow of missionaries going out. But I believe our inner commitment to missions, the sense of how essential they are not only for others' well-being but for our own, has grown weak. Some churches are unsure about evangelism itself. They want to help feed hungry people, or to eliminate injustice, but they suspect proclaiming the gospel to be cultural imperialism. This is radical doubt indeed, for it questions the very validity of Christianity, which has been from the beginning a universal religion—good for everyone or good for no one. You cannot cure such doubts except by returning to the fundamentals and asking fundamental questions.

Other churches, especially evangelical ones, suffer no doubt on this score. They are simply so preoccupied with their own needs and programs that the rest of the world seems only hazily real to them. Missions has become a sideline, an afterthought they support but will not bleed for.

The early mission pioneers of the last century had a very different sense of missions. Many died for it. Few missionaries to Ghana, for instance, lived more than two years from the day they arrived. Yet they came in a continuing wave until the church was established. I do not know whether we could find similar volunteers today.

But Jesus came to seek and to save the lost. If we do not do the same we will wither and die, lacking the power of the risen Jesus. He still seeks and saves the lost, and he will keep on doing so with or without us. May this book serve as an encouragement to those who join him.

1
The Snake
& the Egg

WE LEFT LONDON late at night and flew through the dark hours, mostly over the huge mass of Africa. I did not sleep at all. Our flight stopped in Cairo, and I stared out the jet's tiny window at the airport arc lights creating a tent of bluish light. Then we flew off again. When the sun came up we were following the Nile, a muddy ribbon twisting through sere sand and rock. The vast country showed no roads or buildings. Leaving the river we continued south over parched, brown hills, until finally our altitude began to drop. I saw the spikes of a nest of tall buildings: Nairobi.

I had never felt more excited. What were we to do there? I was to start a magazine. Popie, my wife, was to teach counseling. But how, and in what circumstances, we hardly knew. We had needed to look for Kenya on a map when the possibility of going there first arose.

In our late twenties, we had been out of college and working for six years. Palo Alto, California, adjoining Stanford University, was the town we called home. Long ago, it seemed now, we had left that relaxed, sunny, highly intellectual nexus —a swirl of computer lingo, sweeping hills and vegetarian co-ops. We loved it; we had wept real tears when we drove away.

We knew what we had left but next to nothing about what we were going to, for all that filters through the information media about Africa are stories of military coups and starvation. A few years earlier the papers had printed a photo from Nairobi of Jomo Kenyatta and Henry Kissinger standing with some wildly decorated tribal dancers. Were such dancers in their monkey-fur capes part of Nairobi street scenes or a relic preserved for tourists? We did not know.

Our plane landed and we made our way through customs. A group of smiling Africans and missionaries met us, and we drove to our new home. We stared out the car windows, bug-eyed. Everything looked new. Red clay paths wandered alongside every road, with scores of people walking them. Towering, feathery shapes, tropical trees, stood stained purple or red.

For our first few days we explored. We stared at green and red bananas for sale in the market. Women selling vegetables wore brilliant combinations of colors—an orange sweater, green tennis shoes, a purple scarf, a fire-red skirt. The city streets were crowded with pretty black secretaries in high heels and men in business suits. We saw no tribal dancers, but we could hear a dozen languages in a single coffee shop. Three-piece suits mixed with turbans, and you could occasionally spot an old man with ear-lobe holes you could push a fist through, or a woman balancing a basket on her head.

Soon such sights became ordinary, though. I laughed at myself one day, typing in my office oblivious to a large three-horned chameleon stutter-stepping in the tree outside my window. I had stopped marveling at the marvelous. Gradually we began to sort Nairobi out and to make a life for ourselves in it.

We were surprised to discover the thriving subculture of white people. Besides many missionaries, we found business executives, embassy personnel, UN and government technical experts, anthropologists, game photographers. They live in Nairobi by the thousands, and many hardly seemed aware that they were in Africa. Foreigners in Nairobi and in many other Third World countries may attend parties, eat in restaurants and go to the theater hardly encountering the people whose home country they live in. Many do, in fact, live in Nairobi for years without making an African friend. The only Africans they know are their servants.

This large foreign population is particular to cities like Nairobi. Large, relatively efficient, with a pleasant climate, Nairobi is headquarters for many international organizations. Outside Nairobi white faces only dot a large black canvas.

As we traveled and met many Americans and Europeans living in more remote conditions, however, we noted they were not always much closer to Africans then we in Nairobi. Many depended on other white people for real friendship. They sometimes traveled great distances from one white friend to another, like trapeze artists swinging across a bottomless void by hanging onto one safety bar until the last moment possible, and then letting go for an instant to clutch the next. It seemed to us they were in Africa but not of it. Surrounded by Africans, they maintained a distance from them.

A European Tea Party
We noticed a similar separateness in the old colonial writings —even the very finest, such as Isak Dinesen's *Out of Africa*. "It was not easy to get to know the Natives," she wrote. "They were quick of hearing, and evanescent; if you frightened them they could withdraw into a world of their own, in a second, like the wild animals which at an abrupt movement from you are gone—simply are not there. Until you knew a Native

well, it as almost impossible to get a straight answer from him."[1]

Of course, neither she nor other colonial writers painted Africa as a European tea party. Africans appear constantly in their writings. But they seldom speak, and when they do their words are strange to us, from another world. The authors sometimes compare Africans to animals—lions, snakes, buffalo—or even plants—the somber, silent trees of the forest. These comparisons were not meant to insult. The writers meant to admire a kind of noble wildness. But they implied that whites can no more understand blacks than we can understand wild animals. A profound and impenetrable gap remained.

The old missionaries did considerably better, I believe. They had not come for money, land or adventure, but to preach the gospel. Their message was the same they preached to their own people at home. Naturally, if you want to get across a message of sin and redemption, you have to get personal. You must assume that Africans are people like yourself, filled with contradictory longings and lusts, joys and distress. You must respect them as potential brothers.

Some of these early missionaries still live in the memory of elderly Kenyans, remembered with deep respect and appreciation. Unlike many colonists, the missionaries were fluent in local languages, they visited in Kenyan homes, and they used persuasion rather than force to accomplish what they wanted. These remarkable men and women were responsible for one of the great movements of faith in all history. They gave the gospel to Africa.

Nevertheless, I believe some gap of understanding often remained. How could it have been otherwise? The missionaries had not seen the world on National Geographic specials. They lived in an age with little idea of cultural relativity, an age which judged every culture by the standard of European civilization. They gaped, naturally, at something utterly new. If a thin snake is to swallow a round egg, his jaw must come unhinged. The gaping jaw is evident in some of the old missionary books which describe strange clothes and customs with such relish, as though to emphasize their differentness.

The Africans gaped too. All that European civilization could do, from writing down words to putting on shoes, was like magic to them at first. People with so little common ground must naturally find themselves separated by a gap of understanding.

My grandfather, a missionary for nearly forty years in Pakistan, once told me about a Pakistani pastor who was devoted to him. In the Pakistani Presbyterian General Assembly, this pastor would inevitably glance across the room to see how my grandfather voted. He would then vote the same way. This made my grandfather uneasy, and he made up his mind to talk to him about it. "Pastor, it is not necessary for you to vote the same way I do. You should vote by your own conscience." Ever after, said my grandfather, the pastor would watch him to see how he voted, and then vote the opposite.

I savor this story as a parable of a cultural gap. You cannot divine the precise reason why the pastor votes the same as you, or the opposite; and trying to find out is bound to set off further ripples of misunderstanding. If you ask him, he will think you want to interfere with his vote, and react against what he perceives as your motive. You have no choice but to leave well enough alone. The gap remains. You hope it doesn't interfere with the business at hand.

In Africa (and in many other places) it did not. It is a tribute to men and women on both sides of the gap that respect could bridge such differences and that the gospel could cross over.

The Still-Wide Gap

I went to Kenya expecting to find the gap greatly narrowed, if not gone. Most young Kenyans now go to school. They dress as we do; they ride in cars, work in offices, keep their money in the bank. Many of them grew up going to church just as I did. Furthermore, the era of colonialism is over. Most African countries have been independent for decades. African churches have, likewise, become independent of the missions that formed them. They are run by nationals, who can be quite outspoken. They may and do make decisions without asking the advice of missionaries.

The missionaries I met generally impressed me. They do not as a group match the secular stereotype of failures who, because they couldn't make it at home, went abroad to lord it over poorly educated people. Such missionaries do exist, I fear, but most missionaries I met are creative, well trained, alert and thoughtful. Engaging in a foreign situation has made them think broadly.

Our Kenyan counterparts were equally impressive. We met well-educated, quick-thinking men and women, whose minds and spirits had absorbed the personality of God through deep prayer and meditation. Such people made paternalistic attitudes difficult to maintain.

Yet, considering all that we now have in common, I found the gap far from erased. Certainly it was smaller between missionaries and Africans than between people in business and Africans. The body of Christ brought Africans and Westerners together as equals, regardless of education or managerial skill. My first reaction was great exhilaration as I saw, for the first time in my life, whites and blacks together, seemingly without tension.

But for many missionaries and for many nationals this fellowship went so far and no further. Some missionaries could truthfully say that their closest friends, the people to whom they looked for fun or comfort or relaxed conversation, included Africans. But many missionaries could not say that at all. They worked with Kenyans, but you would not find Kenyans relaxing in their homes after work, nor would you find them relaxing in Kenyans' homes.

To make this particularly alarming, I soon felt myself falling into their pattern. We were fortunate to work with a small mission deeply committed to nationalization, and I couldn't escape, even if I had wanted to, constant working relationships with Kenyans. But when work was done I was tired. Sometimes I was homesick. Though I liked the Kenyans I was meeting, I did not find it easy to be with them because they were so different. It was easier and more restorative to be with people like myself.

I could see, dimly at least, how this might cripple my work. The gospel is a weighty thing, and it must travel on strong bridges of trust. At a purely practical level I needed, as all missionaries need, to understand our hosts' sensibilities; otherwise we could not adapt our work to the local culture. But could we share in this understanding and trust if we could not manage to share in friendship? I had not foreseen this problem before going to Kenya. I had been more concerned about the technical problems of publishing a magazine. But my attention now shifted toward more personal factors.

Missionary Models
Fortunately, Popie and I had some good models. The first, Joyce Scott, had been in Kenya nearly twenty years. She taught us how to love it. She had given her heart to the country: to the wideness of its skies, to the warmth of its homes, to its patterns of speech, even in a lighthearted way to its occasional inefficiences and irritations. She loved Kenya without paternalism. She was not standing back to view it. It had become her country, and if she criticized it she did so in the same reluctant tone you might use, rarely, to criticize your mother. Consequently she had the deepest kind of Kenyan friendships.

Another model came from a Kenyan couple, John and Emi Gichinga. Bright university graduates who worked with the university Christian fellowships, they could spot a paternalistic attitude like a hawk spots a rabbit. I don't think I do them an injustice by saying that they were not by nature drawn to white people; yet inexplicably they befriended us, and through plenty of storms they helped us understand something of the logic of Kenyan thinking—or illogic, as it sometimes seemed at first to us. Their attitude was perhaps more important than the information. They had, I believe, made up their minds that friendship with missionaries was a good thing. They determinedly saw the good, even when our differences frustrated them. In their work with the International Fellowship of Evangelical Students (IFES) and in their lives this teamwork clearly had produced positive results.

A third model came from the recent past. We had become acquainted with the Nakuru Laymen's Association, a group of Kenyan farmers and businessmen who had devoted themselves to wholistic Christian ministry to poor farmers in their area. They spoke with powerful loyalty of a missionary named Thom Hopler, who had been a catalyst to their thinking and doing. The extent to which they had worked as equals and friends is best seen in the fact that, after Hopler's death back in the United States, the Laymen sent two of their members to see his widow, Marsha. Believing themselves responsible for her welfare, they had made arrangements to start a business she could manage. It had not occurred to them to merely receive benefits from the Hoplers. They felt responsible to give.

Yet such partnership was exceptional. It did not happen as a matter of course. Our conversations with the Gichingas and other Kenyans warned us against taking the problem lightly. It would have been easy to overlook, and some missionaries did just that. They saw themselves as having adequate relationships with Kenyans and would get rather touchy at a suggestion that things could be better. Kenyans gave us a different view.

We naturally notice the changes we have made to adapt to a strange culture. The changes we haven't made, we don't notice: you don't hear the sound of your heart beating, you don't see the picture that has always hung on the wall. But our hosts are in just the opposite position. They don't notice the adaptation we *have* made, because this is what is ordinary to them. They feel the parts that remain unchanged—for these parts grate on them.

Children Walking Hand in Hand

Different cultures do not easily mingle, anywhere. Racial integration in the United States has proven far less brotherly than I imagined when I first heard Martin Luther King, Jr., proclaim his dream of children walking hand in hand. In Kenya, or any African country I know of, tribes stay nearly as divided as blacks and whites. One rarely finds a Luo relaxing in a Kikuyu home, though they are both Kenyans. Such divisions are found wherever differing cultures are thrown together.

Communication between two cultures is a delicate and gentle art. Perhaps understanding will always be rare. Yet I think it could be a great deal less rare among Christians, for some of the barriers that keep us apart are really quite weak. Sometimes a single piece of information can make a huge difference.

Our first year in Kenya was a lonely one. We tried hard to make friends with Kenyans and became acquainted with quite a number. We wanted to know them better. How do you signal that to someone? In the United States you invite him or her to dinner. It never occurred to us that another culture might do it differently. But we noticed that our would-be friends became extremely evasive when we tried to fix a date. They seemed so busy we couldn't imagine how they found time for any socializing at all. We had to fix dates weeks in advance. Even then, some would not appear on the appointed day. Others came but seemed strangely nervous. We usually had a good time, but not easily. And it was virtually unrepeatable. When we tried for a second evening together, they evaded us completely, often saying that it was not right for us, as guests in Kenya, to have them to our house before we came to *their* homes.

But we were never invited! We puzzled over that many times. An African who came to work with a Christian organization in the United States would be invited to dozens of meals. But in Kenya, with one or two stilted exceptions, no one invited us home, neither members of Kenya Youth for

Christ (the group we were working with), nor church and fellowship members, nor neighbors. We thought they liked us. Unless we read all the social signals wrong, they appreciated us. But how could we make friends when we only saw people in passing, at church or while on business?

Popie grew up in Tuscaloosa, Alabama, and retains the enthusiastic warmth of the South. She often has trouble with friends—too many of them. Friendships are a crucial element in both our lives, not an afterthought. When we thought of life in Africa, we had thought of making friendships with Africans, not just doing work within the borders of an African country.

But we were frustrated. We felt homesick and lonely. Letters from home seemed few and far between. We wanted African friends, and we needed them. But we did not seem to be making them. Meanwhile we met many interesting people from England and Sweden and Holland, as well as from America. They *did* invite us. We saw how easily and profitably we could fill our whole calendar with them.

But what about Kenyans? Kenyans would never feel comfortable within that set. So we made a rule for ourselves: we would not pursue friendship with any non-African. *Pursue* is the key word, for we did make good non-African friends. But we almost never took any initiative with them. We waited, sometimes feeling quite lonely, to find our way into friendship with Kenyans.

A retired missionary had given me a helpful piece of advice: "Find Africans who will tell you the truth, however unpleasant, and not the truth you want to hear." And eventually some Kenyans did tell us what we were doing wrong. It was simple.

In Kenya and in most African countries, you rarely if ever invite people to your home on a particular date. To do so only confuses them. If you want to become friends with someone, you simply go to his or her home, without any invitation (though it is fine to warn them you are coming). Whether you arrive at a mealtime or not doesn't matter, for at any time of day they will feed you. You should expect to stay for a bare minimum of one hour, and half a day is more like it. You will always be welcome.

Easily said, but not so easily done. In the United States we could drop in on *good* friends (though preferably not at mealtimes), but we would never do it with mere acquaintances. The first few times we stood at the door of Kenyans we didn't know well, and who weren't expecting us, we felt very nervous indeed.

But it worked. They always welcomed us—always, in the warmest way possible. No one ever seemed to be on the verge of going out. (We learned later that, if they were, they canceled their plans.) They fed us, they showed us their family photo albums, they acted pleased we had come. Like magic, such visits opened the door to friendship.

As we visited them, they began to visit us, also without warning and often at mealtimes. We had to adjust, and no doubt we made many offensive mistakes in doing so. But mistakes could be forgiven and corrected. Until we found the way to mix freely, we made few mistakes—and few friends.

An almost impenetrable barrier between cultures had been formed by a simple and small difference of procedure. A single piece of information broke the barrier down. Yet we had found it astonishingly difficult to get that piece of information. Apparently others do too. Just a short time ago I heard of some missionaries in Tanzania who were troubled that Tanzanians had not been friendly to them: "They never invite us to their homes."

The Invisible Plastic Film

I believe most missionaries arrive, as we did, full of enthusiasm, expecting (rather nobly) to plunge into the local culture and people. But they find it difficult to get beneath the surface. The surface seems to be an invisible, tough plastic film. It bends where you plunge, but it does not give. You may even think you have made it in, and later discover you have not at all.

Many give up and resign themselves to the surface. They find their true friends among people like themselves, whether few or many, who dot the map. You can still hear speculative discussions among Westerners, reminiscent of colonialist books, of what "the Africans" are like. Africans, I am told, sometimes hold similar discussions about "the Europeans." This is what I want to counter. My thesis, simply stated, is this: All missionaries, whatever their work, can be more effective if they mix freely with the people they serve.

One missionary on hearing this reacted, "I know of at least two missionaries who spent most of their time relaxing in the homes of African church leaders. Neither missionary was encouraged by the African church leaders to return. These 'younger' missionaries had an American teen-age image of how to make friends, and they were not respected in Africa."

This objection raises an important point. A missionary is not called to make friends. He is called to do some work: to preach, to teach, to train. The quality of this work is what determines his effectiveness, and it determines (usually, though not always—Third World church bureaucracies are no better than ours) whether he is appreciated by the partners he works with. To go overseas thinking that your friendship makes a contribution in itself is at least an adolescent, if not also a paternalistic, attitude.

We go to work. But hard work can be counterproductive in cross-cultural situations if we don't have relationships of trust to build on, or if we don't understand the culture around us. These relationships and these understandings will come mainly, I believe, through friendships—intimate, informal friendships where we appreciate one another as equals. Friendship is not the whole story of missionary effectiveness, but it is one story. And it is the story I intend to tell.

Because of our experience with visiting, I initially thought information was the key. I foolishly set out to compile a small manual for new missionaries in Kenya, telling them about the local culture. The further I carried that project, the more snarled I became. Technical problems abounded: How much detail should I go into? What about the numerous small but significant differences between tribes? Perhaps even greater differences separated urban, educated Kenyans from their brothers and sisters in remote areas. I became weighed down with tons of material, most of it of questionable help to a new missionary. Of course, I also realized that I was in far over my head. I doubt that any individual knows all the cultural variations in Kenya well enough to write such a book. At any rate, I most certainly didn't.

Something else troubled me. All the information I could give was readily available. Anyone who asked Kenyans could learn it in short order. But some people never asked. Or if they did ask, the information didn't seem to perk down to any action on their part. Something more basic than information was needed. What made some people mix? What kept others aloof?

Personality has something to do with it. Some missionaries seemed naturally friendly, flexible, patient. Mixing came easily to them. They might be ignorant of African culture and make many goofs, but they won appreciation because it was clear they meant well. I saw, in contrast, others who, having studied anthropology and communication principles, could give lectures on African culture; but they did not know how to get along.

Information and skill do play a part. An anthropological perspective on culture helps some people accept traits they otherwise would condemn. The skill of curiosity, of asking questions, gives some a method for learning informally. But, by itself, it is inadequate. I came to the conclusion that many factors work together to help those who succeed. If I must name one master ingredient, it is persistence. Those who persist in trying to make friends will nearly always succeed. They will overcome their handicaps.

No one can give you persistence. But understanding the barriers you face can help. That invisible plastic film of culture discourages you by keeping you baffled. How will you penetrate what you can't see? Where will you find the secret? What is wrong? But if the barriers are laid out systematically, you may find that they *can* be crossed, one by one.

In each chapter of this book I will try to outline the shape of one barrier and offer some strategies for getting over it. What I say is necessarily general. I have relied on my African experiences, which others have confirmed are typical. But each culture, each country, is different. Making friends among illiterate, rural people will be different from making friends in the cities. Even if I covered every conceivable cultural variation—an impossible task—it would not be enough. Each individual will react differently from the way others facing precisely the same circumstances would react. This book is not a road map, then, and cannot be. In crossing cultural boundaries you are always an explorer. I can only give you a sense of your ultimate direction—and the encouragement to keep on exploring until you find the friendships you had hoped for.

Sharing a Single Bed

For me, exploring makes the happiest part of living in another culture. Almost every day after work Popie and I came together eager to compare what we had learned. This was exhilarating, humorous, stimulating.

But exploring has its frustrations and humiliations, too. To remain perpetually ignorant, to continue to make mistakes, to accidentally damage friendships wears you down. Just when you begin to think you know your way, you ruin something. Someone who has lived in Africa for thirty years may well feel more at home there than in England or America. But that is because he is out of touch with England and America. I doubt he will ever be taken all the way into Africa.

Walter Trobisch served in Africa for many years. He wrote books like *I Loved a Girl* and *I Married You* with Africa in mind, and they have been remarkably effective there as well as in other parts of the world. No other missionary I know of has managed to communicate so well on such emotional, culture-laden subjects. But I learned in an amusing way that even he made mistakes.

My wife used *I Married You* in teaching a course of marriage and family counseling. The book tells about some talks Trobisch gave in an African city and the personal counseling he did between sessions. In the course of the story his wife arrives from another country, and he realizes that he has not arranged for a hotel room with a double bed. His room has only a single bed, and since all double rooms are taken, his wife is forced to sleep in a separate room. This precipitates a quarrel between them.

My wife's students were puzzled. "But why did he refuse to sleep with his wife?" they kept asking.

Popie could not understand their question. Only after extended discussion did she grasp the problem. She remembered that when we stayed in Kenyan homes, they provided us with one single, narrow bed, a tight squeeze for two. Though her students had been exposed to Western culture more than most, they could not see why a narrow bed would keep a man from sleeping with his wife. They did not, in fact, recognize the bed as the issue at all. They thought Trobisch had simply refused his wife's company. By telling the story, Trobisch had meant to communicate that he and his wife were fallible human beings who also had trouble getting along. But his message backfired. Rather than making himself more human, he had made himself alien and ascetic. What kind of creature refuses to sleep with his wife after such a long absence?

If Trobisch could make such a mistake—tiny, but potentially serious—none of us is exempt from them. This does not excuse ignorance. But it points out that we need more than facts. We need attitudes and understandings that keep us reaching out to people, again and again.

Missionaries do remarkably varied work. Some preach and plant churches. Others translate languages. Still others run computers. But all work outside their own culture, and could work more effectively if they genuinely understood, in heart as well as mind, those they work with. This can only come when people freely associate. It is not enough for us to know that senses of humor differ in different cultures. We must learn to laugh when others laugh, and laugh from the gut. This retraining is hard work. But note well: who doesn't enrich himself who learns how to laugh in a new way?

2
Culture
Fatigue

I DOUBT MANY missionaries step off the plane with plans for keeping their distance. Enthusiastic, their eyes big and bright, they ask questions and eagerly shake hands with everyone. They may be frightened, nervous and ignorant, but they are willing to learn. In fact, many learn more in the first month than they do in the following year. The mind is vulnerable at first.

Some veterans may patronize enthusiasm. They may joke about the eager beavers. But I cannot think of a better quality to begin with. Enthusiasm usually comes with curiosity, and curiosity is just what you need to fill up caverns of ignorance. Of course, new missionaries also come with some negative qualities, particularly a cheerful belief that they have a lot to offer. This makes them both too quick to act and too slow to listen. But on the whole I am optimistic about the kind of people who make missionaries. Most are eager to learn and serve.

The gap develops only later, as they respond to the repulsive force of a strange culture. Culture is more than a barrier. It is a wedge. With every hammer blow it splits people apart.

Everybody knows about culture shock by now, a kind of psychological disease that disorients people who are new in unfamiliar territory. Culture shock happens when you lose all your familiar social cues. Suddenly even the most fundamental interactions, like shaking hands, are confusing. You lose your sense of confidence and may become deeply depressed. Eventually most people begin to understand the new culture they are in, and they may end up actually enjoying some of the same things that earlier immobilized them. They are then over "culture shock."

But the term *culture shock* is not an accurate or complete description of the problem. It implies a sudden, jarring onslaught of culture slamming against you. A shock starts suddenly, and it ends soon after. That is part of the story, but not all. Many people do go through a sudden, deep trough in their first year abroad. But others react in just the opposite way: they feel exhilarated. The new culture frees them from routines that had confined and bored them. New sights and ideas stimulate their creativity. Newness can even be restful, which is why people go away from home for vacations.

So some people escape culture shock. But no one, I think, eludes culture *fatigue.* In every vacation, a time comes when you want to return home. Little things, which perhaps seemed exciting at first, begin to eat at you. The predictable routines of home life sound seductive rather than dull. You look forward to knowing that your underwear is in the third drawer on the left; you have tired of hunting through your suitcase for it.

That is a small portion of what missionaries experience. Whether a strange culture is a pleasant or unpleasant shock, it wears you down. You get tired of unfamiliarity and uncertainty. The fatigue is usually worst in your first one or two years, but it may persist much longer. Culture fatigue moves like a glacier, pushing you steadily away from the people you want to befriend. Time after time you feel too tired to make the effort to relate to them.

Different people find different things tiring. Many Americans who work in Kenya, for instance, are bothered by the elasticity of time. Meetings that start late rub them the wrong way. But this never bothered me at all. What drove me nearly insane were the telephones, which worked no more than fifty per cent of the time. Eventually I adjusted enough to wearily accept them, but the irritation always lurked just under my skin.

The Varieties of Repulsion

Every missionary can, I suppose, cite his own peculiar difficulties. T. Wayne Dye, working in Papua New Guinea, writes,

> The Bahinemo viewpoint on caring for dogs was a source of resentment to me for years. They will not kill any dogs because of their belief in a dog's afterlife. As a result, the dogs multiply until there are more than can be fed in their subsistence economy. Only puppies and good hunting dogs are fed. The others are kept away from the family's food by frequent kicking and clubbing. Some dogs slowly starve. I hold an opposite value: a dog should either be fed and cared for or put out of its misery.[1]

This difference in values was a constant, wearing irritant to Dye. Edith Norwood, a missionary in South America, writes of what disturbed her:

> I never overcame my horror at the cruelty of the people around me toward animals and people, especially the helpless, maimed and handicapped. Insane and retarded people roam the streets and are *constantly* subject to jeers and physical abuse. I have seen a gang of boys beat a low-flying pelican out of the sky with sticks and club it to death "just for fun." One night a group of revelers found a beautiful little sick dog in the street outside our garden gate and played "futbol" (soccer) with it until it was kicked to death.[2]

These are obvious extremes. More subtle factors may be just as wearing, however.

Purely physical factors put great stress on some people. Mothers worry about health hazards for their children. The daily sight of cockroaches in the kitchen or lizards in the living room may wear you down. Running out of water or having to use pressure lamps when you are used to unlimited electricity will seem intolerable to some. (Others take it as fun, "just like camping"—at least for a while.)

Your personality may cause problems. Shy people, Dye notes, were consistently troubled by the boisterous and affectionate personalities of most New Guinea Highlanders. Perhaps Popie should have gone there. She likes to touch people affectionately and found it hard to accept that in Kenya she had to keep her hands to herself.

But it is not one problem, usually. Many problems, each one small in itself, conspire together to wear you down. A web of differences binds you. You feel frustrated and unhappy, and you may not even be sure just why.

Of course, some cultures are more "different" than others. Going to Papua New Guinea requires bigger adjustments than going to, say, England. But a culture relatively similar to your own may prove just as wearying, simply because trouble is unexpected. Some of the unhappiest situations result when missionaries from similar but subtly different cultures are thrown together. Dye mentions that in Papua New Guinea Australian missionaries are known to value a cautious use of money, while American missionaries value time and will spend money like water to save time. When they work together, their different approaches may lead to bitter feelings.

A knowledge of anthropology will not necessarily alleviate culture fatigue. In fact, someone who has studied anthropology may at times have the hardest adjustment of all. He understands cultures and may expect his understanding to translate into experience. He may plan to become totally immersed in his new host culture. His pride tells him that he must, but he finds in experience that he cannot. This message of failure and frustration is underlined a hundred times a day. Paul Buttrey writes this from Taiwan:

I have had the image in my mind that at some point I would be able to almost completely identify with the people I was ministering to. The longer we are here, the more I realize how unChinese I really am. There are great cultural gaps between the Eastern and Western worlds which I doubt can be fully overcome by many people. In fact, most students of missions feel that if a person identifies too heavily with the host culture ("goes native") he loses something of himself in the process and will develop serious psychological and spiritual problems. There must be a balance. . . . I think we are trying to find this balance right now. For example, we like to have people over, but don't know what foods to serve them. Like any specialized cuisine, Chinese cooking is hard to learn to do well. Do we try to serve them mediocre Chinese food? Do we serve them Western food? This is a trivial example, but multiplied many times over makes us feel uneasy.

We have lost many things which gave us comfort and support in the U.S.A. Our relatives and old friends are no longer around us. All the places we used to enjoy working and playing in have been replaced by unfamiliar places. We cannot engage in old familiar pastimes: working around the yard, watching TV, playing squash. We aren't as mobile as we were at home. There we could hop in a car and go wherever we wanted. Here we must rely on a bus, a taxi, or bicycles. I cannot adequately describe the exhilaration I felt when I had an opportunity to drive a car for the first time in Taiwan; it was a thrilling experience!

These differences in lifestyle (and many others, which we may not be aware of) affect us at a very deep level. Sometimes we don't even understand the forces at work on us. We find that we are quite emotionally unstable. One day we will feel pretty good. The next day we will feel quite depressed for no apparent reason. We often feel that we have no extra energy. When we return home from class, all we can do is collapse on the bed.

Others under the same circumstances would react to different aspects of Taiwan. I cannot imagine myself exhilarated, under any set of circumstances, by a chance to drive a car. But I might be irritated by something the Buttreys did not even notice.

Correct Facts, Wrong Conclusions

Living in Nairobi is unquestionably easier than living in, say, the Turkana region of Kenya—remote, undeveloped, terribly hot, infested with poisonous spiders and populated by nomads who, since they have little or no school experience, may seem to have virtually nothing in common with an American. Someone living in those conditions may feel reasonable resentment toward anyone who suggests that his cultural identification could be greater. But differences in culture are not easy for anyone, and I suspect the strongest pressures are generally the least exotic: simple loneliness, the feeling of helplessness, the loss of small comforts and good conversations. The net effect of many nagging discomforts is rarely overwhelming, except that the pressure is constant. You have to cope with it somehow. How do you?

One solution is orientation. The new culture confuses you; nothing works the way you expect. The sooner you understand, the sooner you will feel better. In recent years many mission groups have realized they need better orientation for new staff, and so they require classes, some quite extensive, to help you understand and adapt.

While these classes are worthwhile, my impression is that they have limited effectiveness. The reason is simple. Such courses are theoretical. Practical, on-the-field education always carries far greater weight. In most missions, massive practical orientation begins the moment a missionary reaches his new home. His fellow missionaries educate him.

A new missionary can hardly resist the flat assertion made by a veteran that "you'll get a lot more done if you do it this way." Your fellow missionaries will tell you where to live, whether to hire servants, how much to pay, where to buy food, how to prepare food, whether and how to boil water, where to shop, how to deal with the government bureaucracies, how to go about your work, how to dress, what to buy and, above all else, what to expect from local people.

Much of this information is of tremendous practical help. Many missionaries will affirm, "We would never have made it if the Joneses hadn't taken us under their wings." But there is a problem. Local culture is seldom explained entirely sympathetically, in a way that local people would express it to each other. This local view is what you need so much to know if you are to do more than survive, if you are to adapt and mingle freely. You need to know how your hosts themselves see and express the facts of their culture. Otherwise you may agree on facts but have absolutely no meetings of minds.

Let me give an example.

My daughter Katie was born in Kenya, and when Popie was pregnant we asked some close Kenyan friends about breast feeding. Educated Kenyan women rarely breast-feed babies for long, perhaps because nearly all of them work. We had not seen others in our social network breast-feed their children and were uncertain whether it would be acceptable in public. So we asked whether people might be offended.

Our friends thought about it for a little while. "No, I don't think so. In fact, it would be good. People would be surprised."

"Why is that?"

"Some people would be surprised that you want to be so close to the baby."

"But why would that surprise them?"

"Well, you know, we tend to think that white people don't like children."

"But why would you think that?"

They had to think. "I don't really know why. Maybe because you people brought birth control, and since you don't want to have children you probably don't like them."

I should add that this conversation occurred with a couple who had done advanced degrees at the University of California at Berkeley. I found, in checking, that most Kenyans agreed: white people do not like children. And, in a certain way, they are correct. We do not like children to inconvenience us. We do not like them to disrupt our careers or our marriages or our financial plans. We do not like them, then, in the way that most Kenyans do. For Kenyans, as far as I can understand it, babies are just *good*. They need not be good for anything; they are, at a fundamental, unexplainable, nonfunctional level, filled with blessing. Why would anyone want to limit such blessing or put it off? Babies are the best thing that can happen. Our behavior, our fascination with birth control, continually bewilders them.

I mention this case because, when we hear ourselves described from their angle, we see how mistaken information based on facts can be. Yet I think Kenyans know more about us than we do about Kenyans.

Kenyans would be terribly shocked and offended to hear Westerners say that they do not care for their babies—which Westerners do say. Kenyans care for them, worry over them, sometimes smother them with care—but in their way, and not ours. By my lights, Kenyans go wrong leaving the children at home with illiterate girls from the countryside, of whom they have not a single character reference. These girls are notorious for their lack of honesty, good sense and reliability.

But that is my way of looking at it. A Kenyan has a different view. He sees that I do not dress my child warmly, that I allow her to suck her thumb and that I sometimes let her cry herself to sleep; he is sure that I do not care for her.

With such a great gulf between our cultures, we can probably never completely meet each other. We will always see things from different angles. However, we can come closer and at least get our information from the right people. Our fellow Westerners will volunteer information more freely and will give it in a package that makes a tidy kind of sense to us. But we should beware of formulations. We should beware of quick conclusions.

Bonding: Babies and Missionaries

Should, then, new missionaries receive no information or help whatsoever from fellow missionaries? This radical approach is suggested by Thomas and Elizabeth Brewster in their excellent and challenging booklet *Bonding and the Missionary Task*.[3] They believe a new missionary can "bond" to a culture just as a newborn animal (or child) bonds to his or her parents just after birth. Timing is critical, the Brewsters say, and so they suggest that missionaries decide before coming (and request cooperation from their mission agency) to utterly avoid Western contacts during their first few months in a country. Otherwise, they will bond to other Westerners and view the local culture from their distant, critical perspective. Later, say the Brewsters, the new missionaries may wish to make Western friends, but by that time they will be bonded to their host culture—that is, they will be comfortable in it and find most of their needs met by it.

The Brewsters suggest that new missionaries bring no more than twenty kilos of possessions—the maximum the airlines let you carry—and immediately plunge into learning the language by making systematic contacts with local people. They further suggest that you immediately ask new contacts if they know a family you can move in with for a few months! And you should use nothing but local transportation. This total involvement, the Brewsters say, results in many friendships and in greatly reduced culture shock. The brand new missionary, excited and highly alert, will never again be so able to adapt as in those first weeks.

This bonding approach, being new, will need to be thoroughly evaluated over time. It may not be for everybody. Most missionaries will probably continue to find their arrival cushioned by the well-meant help of other missionaries. I am not sure this is all bad, or that timing is so utterly crucial as the Brewsters suggest. After all, to turn the tables around, most foreign students enter the United States without any help from non-Americans, yet those who work with foreign students say that a high percentage develop deep isolation and leave America repelled by everything American. Bonding does not come as a matter of course for them, and it will not for us. What makes the Brewsters' approach so effective, I suspect, is that it bonds the new missionary to a firm commitment to overcome cultural barriers. It is awkward to back away from such a radical beginning. You set your direction; you won't unconsciously change.

I do feel certain that the bonding approach hits one crucial point. You must not let a network of Western friends become a net that catches and binds you or a veil that permanently blinds you. Let it be at most a starting point. From the beginning set your direction beyond that network. You may have to deliberately cut yourself free from it.

If you study physics, you begin with a simple, generalizing textbook aimed at beginners. You should know, however, that the mysteries of physics are more complex and that what you learn is, while not false, not precisely true either. You aim to someday reach a higher level. So it is with information from your fellow Westerners. Take it for what it is worth, but remain skeptical. Look for opportunities to learn better from your hosts. You will only do this by making friends, and, paradoxically, you will only make friends by doing this. For understanding is at the root of any real friendship.

Something Worth Working For

It takes energy. Making friends across cultures requires time and work and frustration. Understanding does not turn on like a light. But at the end is unparalleled satisfaction. You are bringing into being, in a partial way, the climax of history.

"I looked and there before me was a great multitude that no

one could count, from every nation, tribe, people and language, standing before the throne and in front of the Lamb" (Rev 7:9). The very diversity of language and culture in that crowd makes a shout of acclamation, proof of God's overwhelming power to break every barrier.

The barrier of culture is not high, but it is wide. It is an obstacle more like a marsh than a deep chasm. You can easily cross a bit of it, but it is hard to keep on going because your legs get dead weary from the mud. At the end, though, is that scene from Revelation. And even before the end come moments of profound though quiet revelation. In the unspectacular unity of different people is the Lord's power, not human power.

I think of some of the missionaries I have known, or known of: of Donald Banks, for many years the sole white face at Africa Christian Press in Ghana, a slight, bemused figure who would, no doubt, offer a burglar a cup of tea out of politeness. He gently trained and brought into being a completely Africanized publishing firm, and then quietly left when his work was done.

I think of Lorna and Betty, two single women in Kenya who drove into the Masai manyattas night after night, year after year, to befriend people who showed little interest in the good news they were telling. Now, twenty years later, Lorna and Betty are watching others reap the seed they planted.

I think of Margaret Burt, who goes for weeks at a time without speaking a word of English and prefers to keep doing so though she is long past retirement. As she told me, her family in Scotland is gone; her real family is Kenyan. In fact, she admits, Kenyans brought her to a dynamic faith during the great East Africa Revival, even though she was already a veteran missionary. Perhaps that explains why partnership comes naturally to her. She has received from those she serves.

A letter from friends in Singapore has come today as I make final corrections on this manuscript. New missionaries, they write, "The last eighteen months have been very tumultuous for us. We've left stability, familiarity and normalcy behind.

We have a strong conviction of God's will in being here, which is carrying us over the rough places. (I think they're larger than spots!) I don't by nature have an adventurous or adaptable personality. I'm sure learning that God doesn't necessarily lead you according to your natural inclinations."

In those upbeat words I detect the residue of some lonely, depressed and frustrated days. But I also detect the seeds of great hope. "God doesn't necessarily lead you according to your natural inclinations." That is more than the seed of hope; it is the seed of a new creation.

It is hard to accept, not only when we become Christians but all through our Christian lives, that our natural inclinations lead only downward: to the unhappy isolation of being left alone to do our own will. To rise to heaven is to be stripped of our possessions, our will, our pride. "Nothing in my hand I bring; Simply to Thy cross I cling; Naked, come to Thee for dress; Helpless, look to Thee for grace."[4] This process does not occur only in prayer meetings; it happens in the weary battering of life.

But what joy is on the other side! Having stripped off our old clothes, we can put on clean ones, hot from the dryer. "For the perishable must clothe itself with the imperishable, and the mortal with immortality. . . . Therefore, my dear brothers, stand firm. Let nothing move you. Always give yourselves fully to the work of the Lord, because you know that your labor in the Lord is not in vain" (1 Cor 15:53, 58).

"You have come to . . . the city of the living God. You have come to thousands upon thousands of angels in joyful assembly, to the church of the firstborn, whose names are written in heaven" (Heb 12:22-23). We don't yet see this assembly, except in embryonic form. But being a missionary across cultures means bringing this diverse assembly into being, joining others in a new family, in a new way of thinking. God doesn't necessarily lead you according to your natural inclinations. He leads you to something you would never have dreamed of.

3
Bridging the Chasm of Culture

WHEN WE HAD BEEN in Kenya for about a year, my wife and I spent Christmas in a rural part of the country. White people cannot often have stayed in that area, for we were a great novelty. Our hosts treated us splendidly. Every home we visited fed us to nose level. Church elders ushered us to the best seats and invited us to address the congregation. Anyone who met us on village paths stopped to greet us and showed great interest in our welfare.

When we were preparing to leave, our host made a comment I found vaguely disturbing. "My people have enjoyed having you here. They have watched you very closely, and now they believe that you are good people. They want you to know they will be happy if you return another time."

His tone suggested that the message was significant, so I asked him to explain. "People here are very suspicious," he said. "Some thought you might be spies."

Surprised, I puzzled over that response for sometime. They had been so friendly, as had all Kenyans we had met. Could such warmth really mask a deep and irrational suspicion?

Africans Look at Missionaries

But over the next few years, as we developed deeper friendships and Kenyans talked to us more openly, I saw that their friendliness did not mean precisely what we had thought. Kenyans were not deceitful. Their welcome was sincere, for they are a sincerely hospitable people. But they maintain a deeper reserve, and they will not give themselves fully to you until they have watched you a long time. As they are more cordial and polite than we, we can easily misread them. I had to learn to listen more carefully, alert to the slightest shadow of reservation. Only by responding to their doubts and suspicions could we hope to close the gap between us.

When I began thinking about this book, I started making it a practice to ask friends, both missionaries and Africans, what they thought of each other. I found the two groups not always seeing the relationship in the same way.

Most missionaries liked and appreciated Africans, and felt liked and appreciated in return. Their reservations usually fell on questions of culture and ethics: "Why do they do the things that they do?"

Africans varied in their responses quite a lot. Some, especially the better educated, could be quite fierce in their evaluation of missionaries. Others, particularly those in rural settings, seemed extremely grateful. Some of this was their habitual politeness. When I dug deeper, I found in both pro-missionary and antimissionary groups a divided response. They liked some things about us. They strongly disliked other things.

If you asked the average American non-Christian what he thinks of missionaries, he might divide his response between the people and the work. Missionaries themselves, he might admit, are fine people—not necessarily the kind he would invite to a party, but certainly the kind he would be happy to have for neighbors. He would be more likely to hold reservations about the work they do. Why do they have to foist their religion on poor, underdeveloped people? If they must help them, why not give them things they really want, like food and shelter and agricultural advice?

The Africans I talked to make nearly the opposite distinction. Even those you might call antimissionary give credit for good work. No group can match the missionary record for meeting material needs. Most of the hospitals and schools and many of the roads in Africa were built by missionaries. When you travel to arid regions in search of agricultural centers or water projects, you are more likely to find missionaries at the source than the United Nations. Missionaries are known to be honest, reliable and morally upright. Of course, there are always complaints, but these are marginal to the main pattern of good work done in the service of people. Most important, of course, missionaries have with great success spread the news of Jesus Christ. To a non-Christian American this may be foisting something unwanted on people, but Africans are not so likely to see it that way. Millions of Christians, at any rate, are indeed grateful that missionaries came.

But when Africans spoke openly to me of the missionaries themselves, as people, the tune changed. At the least they would say that missionaries puzzled them. And for many, *"un*like" led to *"dis*like." They thought of missionaries as distant, standoffish—negative qualities to sociable Africans. Some of the fiery ones might use words like *proud, insensitive.* Friendlier Africans might simply say, "We believe they are brothers in Christ, but we do not understand why they keep to themselves." They thought of this unpleasant side as an unavoidable aspect of the good work they did—like rainy weather, a mixture of unfortunate necessity with blessing. Oddly enough, even some who had become close friends with one or more missionaries tended still to speak this way of missionaries *in general.* One of my friends, Haron Wachira, wrote me,

I don't know whether you will be surprised when I tell you I have never thought of you and Popie as missionaries. If I had I guess our relationship might have taken a different path. Maybe somehow we would still have managed to break through the barriers of culture to form a deep relationship, but I doubt if it would have been the same.

I should think that attitude is quite typical. George tells me it is the same with him and Rev. Dodman, who is quite close to him. When he tries to think of him as a missionary (even though he knows he is a missionary) he sees a different, more impersonal, superficial relationship.

Are Missionaries Good or Bad?

What is my point in telling this? Certainly not to prove that missionaries are "bad." That is what our non-Christian American might expect: to him missionaries have been busybodies whom intelligent Africans would naturally resent. By the secular stereotype, a missionary at work is terribly distasteful in comparison with, say, wonderfully high-minded embassy officials or newspaper journalists.

I have not found Africans making this distinction. They usually lump all foreigners together. If they had to choose they would probably prefer missionaries by a good margin, for at least missionaries do some tangible good, make an effort to meet Africans and do not behave immorally. (Since missionaries have far more contact with ordinary people than do World Bank officials, however, missionaries may catch more objections.)

The basic problem, I believe, has little to do with whether missionaries are good or bad, saints or charlatans. It even has little to do with whether World Bank officials are good or bad. The problem is that we come from a different culture. Differing cultures do not naturally like each other. They frequently misunderstand each other, reading the worst into each other's motives.

I was sitting at lunch with some Kenyan friends once, and I

listened to them talk laughingly about an attempt to visit one of their Kenyan neighbors. He had built an eight-foot wall around his property, with broken shards of glass ringing the top and a huge metal gate. On going to visit him, they had knocked and banged and shouted until they were hoarse, and no one even heard them.

"Suppose," I asked them, "that you went to Britain and found such a wall when you tried to visit? What stories would you tell when you came home?"

They admitted they would tell the story to prove that the British were cold, isolated and unfriendly. They would not generalize about their fellow Kenyans based on one such experience, but they would about the British. Because the British are different and have the reputation among Kenyans for unfriendliness, they would quickly add the story as "proof." (Of course, we do the same. I have been ashamed to find myself talking about the dominance of bribery in Africa when, in fact, I have only on two or three occasions been asked for a bribe.) This tendency is no doubt sinful, but I think we must face it as a fact about how human beings normally respond to people who are different. In other words, missionaries start off at a disadvantage. A barrier already exists, which we individually had nothing to do with making, but which we are responsible to break down.

I did not find the majority of missionaries aware of this. Americans especially tend to assume (wrongly) that "everybody likes us," just because people are nice to us. This is probably because we have limited experience with really different cultures. We tend to blithely say, "People are all the same under the skin." They are, but you will not reach them at that level without breaking through the barrier of culture.

The Other Side of the Barrier
Of course, there are two sides to the barrier. At least most missionaries try to understand and sympathize with the culture they enter. No one expects our hosts to do the same with

us. Is that fair?

Our hosts do not even want to learn to sympathize. They see the West as pushing itself on their people, undermining their traditional values. To sympathize with the point of view of a Westerner has become something like cultural treason.

As an American I would never fear that, in sympathizing with an African point of view, I might fall into it and never escape. I may adapt to African ways, but I will never lose my sense of Americanness. But an African is bound to feel the danger of assimilation. Others, friends of his, have disappeared down that hole. Many families have a member who is, as they say, "lost in America." They feel, especially if they are educated, the threat that a Western tide will wash away everything distinctively African. In keeping their distance from missionaries, they cling to their own cultural identity.

Another reason why our hosts don't sympathize with us is more commonplace: why should they? By common belief, guests follow the pattern of their hosts. You eat the food that is served you and say thank you. This is common courtesy. Westerners ought to feel shame that we have so often reversed those roles. We have demanded that our hosts adopt our customs, our way of thinking. When they do not leap to do so, we call them uncivilized, or inefficient (a more modern insult).

I am not quite saying that our hosts shouldn't sympathize with us. Perhaps they would be more Christian if they did. Ultimately, the roles of guest and host do not mean much when you realize that we are neither; we are servants.

But on this earth, servant-hearted people are rare. Sometimes you find someone who unaccountably sympathizes with your struggles to adapt to his culture. But you can't count on finding such people, any more than Chinese coming to America can count on everyone to provide chopsticks. Our hosts will not much sympathize with us. It is up to missionaries to fit in, as guests, and to break down the barriers of culture. Here are some more specific suggestions for doing so:

1. Find a sponsor. South America Mission suggests that all its new missionaries find a "sponsor"—someone respected in the local community (a business executive, teacher or other professional) who will watch for and honestly correct their mistakes in social contacts, business and language. You can formalize such a relationship, and arrange for regular meetings. This helps you go beyond Western information. (In a rural setting you may find no one with the education to fit this description. But every community has its respected members, whether educated or not.)

There are two problems with this excellent arrangement. First, respected people are busy. People with time to help—school kids, young people addicted to foreign culture, uneducated workers—may be less capable of acute observations. Your host culture is not uniform! Some people in it can help you much more than others.

Second, in many cultures criticism is muted because directness is impolite. You may be told you are doing very well when it fact you need to make drastic changes. You may not even realize your sponsor is correcting you when he does it indirectly and cautiously. He will think you are refusing to change and grow frustrated. But even then he will rarely tell you so. For a sponsor program to work well, you need the right person, you need to meet often enough to develop real rapport, and you need to grasp enough of the local culture to understand what he is saying.

2. Set specific goals. Many people are encouraged to persist in learning a new culture when they can measure some form of progress. For instance, you can decide to have four extended conversations and fifty slight interactions in a week, and check them off as they occur. (The Brewsters' LAMP program [Language Acquisition Made Practical], which systematizes learning a language through informal, personal contacts, suggests that you make fifty initial contacts in a single day. The "text" a beginner starts with is a greeting, an expression of the desire to learn the language, and the statement that this is all you know how to say, but that you will see them again. You say thank you and good-by and move on to another person. But the ice is broken.)

You can set a goal of visiting five homes in a week or walking through every part of the city you are in during a month. You can make a list of questions about the local culture and systematically find the answers. (*Survival Kit for Overseas Living,* by L. Robert Kohls, has an excellent list of fifty questions.) Thus, although you feel lost in a sea of strangeness, you will be able to see that you are making progress.

3. Push yourself to the limits.[1] A foreign culture is frightening because it is unknown and you feel helpless. But when you throw yourself into it, and at its mercy, you usually survive. Almost invariably, people come out of the woodwork to help you. From then on you're less afraid. You learn a great deal in a short time.

The Overseas Missionary Fellowship, for instance, encourages its missionaries to live in the home of a local family for a time. Those who do often emerge with noticeably fewer problems relating. Unfortunately, it is much more difficult for families to take this course than single people.

When Popie and I had been in Kenya for a short time, we went to a remote area of Kenya to stay with a Kenyan family over the Christmas holidays. While it would have seemed odd to stay with a Kenyan family (whose houses are usually crowded) in the city, under holiday circumstances it was understandable to all. That stay was a breakthrough for us; we never again felt intimidated venturing into all sorts of places. And we had so delightful an experience that we did the same thing year after year, each time learning new things we could never have learned otherwise.

The Option of Escape

There is another way to cope with culture fatigue and alienation: escape.

Paul Buttrey, whose adjustment to life in Taiwan was difficult, related in one of his prayer letters a visit he and his wife paid to a restaurant that served pizza. "When we got home," he wrote, "we mentioned how refreshed we felt after having eaten that familiar food. Having a bit of the United States around us uplifted us."

Two things strike me about this scrap of correspondence. One is how malleable culture is, ultimately. What was it that seemed to them like "a bit of the United States"? Pizza. Apple pie may be American, but pizza was foreign food just a few years ago. I doubt if my grandfather would have felt comforted by it as a "familiar food." But it has become comforting over the years. We can all find hope in this. What is strange now may become homey in time.

But in the meantime, surrounded by strange things, we look for escape routes. Did you notice the language Buttrey used? "Refreshed" and "uplifted," in the language of prayer letters, are more often applied to prayer meetings than to pizza. But I have no doubt they are just the right words. I have no doubt that pizza did more to refresh and uplift than ten prayer meetings would have at that moment. Culture fatigue is not a spiritual problem, though it may take such dimensions. It is a body and mind problem, like seasickness. And relief lies in such practical escapes as pizza, American films, letters from home, a radio that can pull in Voice of America, or the American Women's Association.

But here we reach the danger, planted as usual in the center of refreshment and uplift: the snake in the garden. Culture fatigue means constantly having your nose thrust into something unpleasant. But there is nearly always a way to escape it. Indeed, you need to escape it; you may not survive if you don't. But you may find it far easier, in the end, to escape culture fatigue completely by escaping the culture you are supposed to minister to. While the local culture works on repelling you, other forces attract you toward a happy, separated life. Here is a partial list of ways you can escape:

1. The Mission Compound. In the olden days missionaries

often built a compound where all missionaries lived. They had good reasons for compounds—they needed safety, a healthy water supply, generators, mutual encouragement and opportunity for teamwork. Often they built a school, hospital and church on the compound, along with housing. A wall or high hedge circled the whole.

The atmosphere of a missionary compound is unmistakable. A city may have grown around it, but within you find grass and flowers, peace and quiet, a dreamy regularity of business, and often a fine scenic view. Though the reasons they were built are usually outmoded, these places still exist, and fairly often a new missionary—particularly one involved with medical, educational or administrative work—is simply assigned to live on one. After all, the mission owns the housing and so does not have the expense of rent. The facilities are unmistakably superior to the alternatives. The mission work is centered there. And above all, This Is The Way It Is Done.

Mission compounds have plenty of tensions of their own and may drive as many missionaries off the mission field as culture fatigue does. But the tensions are familiar ones and are therefore extremely seductive. It takes less energy to chafe behind the walls than to go outside and inflict yourself with the unknowns of a foreign culture.

2. *The Busy Social Schedule.* In Nairobi live literally thousands of other Westerners: missionaries, UN representatives, business people, embassy staff, anthropologists and wildlife photographers. They are nice people, interesting people. They invite you over. You invite them back. They invite you to parties, where you meet more of them. They invite you on weekend sightseeing trips. They play tennis. They jog. They have clubs and organizations. They sponsor worthwhile projects. They offer more than enough social life to keep anyone quite busy, and it is all fine, worthwhile and easy to fit into. Making friends with Kenyans is far more difficult, and it requires not doing some things that you enjoy very much—not going to see wild animals, for instance, because Kenyans virtually never do.

Some missionaries get too busy with each other to develop deep relationships outside themselves. To a surprising degree this seems to be true even of those working in rural circumstances, where other Westerners are rare. There, educated local people are also rare, and the cultural gulf is thus much wider. When you feel lonely you can make a lot of a single friend, even one who lives a hundred miles away. And that friend is likely to be a fellow Westerner, rather than one of your hosts, unless you determine differently.

A busy social schedule can help you escape loneliness, but ultimately you will also escape from the people you have come to meet.

3. *The Godfather Complex.* Most missionaries are, in some way, rich. In most cases they have money and organizational skills that none of their hosts can match. If they go to relatively wealthy countries, they may be psychologically more stable and biblically better educated than those they minister to. A missionary may feel that he is terribly needed, that he alone holds the world together. Everyone he encounters is needy. Everywhere he goes his advice is asked. (If not, he can see that it should be.) His car carries people to the hospital; money from his home church pays his coworkers. He becomes a kind of godfather to all. This relieves his cultural disequilibrium. He knows his duties. He has a niche. He can prove his worth by showing all the people he is helping.

The local people may even encourage this. They may want a godfather. When we first went to look for housing, some Kenyans warned us against living in an area known as Buru Buru; it would be too dangerous for whites, they said. Later we came to see that this was not true; in fact, we ended up in a similar area and enjoyed it very much. But local people may put whites and missionaries into a certain social niche too.

In some areas of Latin America the "patron/peon" system remains strong. "It is very easy," Edith Norwood writes, "for missionaries . . . purporting to fight the corrupt system to set themselves up as beneficent 'Patrones' so that Christians become their peones." What is wrong with such beneficence? Simply this: From such a niche you will find it hard to understand the culture in which you are living. You stay on another level. To learn, you need relationships that are equal.

I am not speaking against helping others. You must, of course, do so. Nor is a defined role necessarily bad. It can make people more comfortable with you if they know what you do. But you must beware of letting your beneficent role become a means of escape. Those who depend on you are unlikely to correct you. You need to know people who feel themselves to be on your level, people who will talk to you straight.

4. Work. The majority of missionaries arrive with a strong desire to accomplish something great. If they have raised financial support, this sense is stronger, because they feel duty-bound to earn those gifts. I often felt the weight of my supporters, though I cannot think of a more understanding and supportive group. They had contributed many thousands of dollars. What if I failed them? I could not stand the thought of going home to tell them.

So there is a built-in tendency to bury yourself in your work. With cultural disorientation this can grow far stronger. When you feel lost and uncertain of your identity, getting some work done reassures you. You are, after all, a normal and capable person. Your work proves it. But burying yourself in work may really mean hiding from the people you came to work with—even if your work involves them directly.

For one thing, many Westerners combine a strong work ethic with cultural pride. "Nothing gets done around here if we don't start the ball rolling," we say. This makes us feel superior to the culture we are so disoriented by; it superficially helps us cope. But, of course, the attitude is always communicated, and it alienates the very people we purport to help.

Second, the syntax of work is Western: arrive on time, accomplish tasks, plan for the future, and eliminate wasted time and effort.[2] This leaves little time for relaxed discussion. Granted, the rest of the world has learned that this syntax is proper for "work." But that does not mean they count it their own. At home they may function under different values which we may never discover, even working side by side.

Typically, we propose an agenda and then work hard to accomplish it. At the end of the day we can report certain activities. Having worked hard, we feel better about ourselves. We feel secure to go home and "be ourselves." We want to relax, safe in the knowledge that from 8:00 to 5:00 we did what we came for. We know our supporters will be satisfied.

But we are not working to help our supporters. We are working to help our hosts. They will not be satisfied. They may not so easily detach a person from his or her job. If we are not their partners at home as well as at work, they will perhaps not feel we are partners at all. They will keep their distance because we have kept ours. They will never tell us the cultural secrets we need to make our work a success.

Real success, particularly in Christian missionary work, depends on fitting your work to the way people feel. For instance, a Kenyan once told me that an evening church service would never succeed in Kenya, because Kenyans think of worship as something you do in the morning. If you set your goals on establishing an evening service, you may be continually frustrated no matter how hard you work. This frustration may even make you angry and rude with your hosts.

Many missionaries work hard and appear to accomplish a lot. They are full of plans and strategies. But some plans and strategies need constant propping up because they do not fit the local context. They don't fit, and don't work, because the missionary works too hard. He has used work to fill his time, and it has become an escape from the people he came to serve. He does not understand them, and so his work is not fruitful.

Some Good Escape Routes
Having warned against various forms of escape, I must say something in its favor. The way to overcome the barrier of culture, ultimately, is to "hang in there." If you endure

long enough, refusing to isolate yourself, you will eventually adapt.

In the meantime, escape can be helpful. Wayne Dye writes, "During our first two years in a village, my wife and I never seemed to complete enough work during a week to 'justify' taking time off on Saturdays. The work was burdensome and progress was poor. Finally we decided to take hikes in the forest every Saturday 'for the children's sake,' even though our week's work was not complete. We soon found that significantly more work was getting done in five days than we had been doing in six."

Dye makes the point that actual, physical escape helps. But what you escape from makes a difference. If your ordinary living situation is in the thick of the local culture, then escaping occasionally for a film, a hike, a pizza or a visit to fellow Americans may prove refreshing. These brief escapes may enable you to return home refreshed. Joyce Scott writes,

> Seeing the need for forays back into one's own culture, and taking them consciously for one's sanity, is very different from what [Thomas] Brewster calls "the foray approach," where from the security of the missionary compound the missionary makes occasional forays into the African world to do his thing, and returns home to base feeling he's done it and can now relax and write his prayer letters with a good conscience. If he is really living where the people live and finding most of his refreshment there, including having his spiritual and social needs met by the church people, it will be fun and very healthy to move out one night a week or one weekend a month into his own group and "come up for air" before going back.

The form of escape also makes a difference. For instance, Dye chose to hike. Surely a day in the forest was less alien to his host culture than an evening at the American club. You can imagine inviting a new, local friend along on the hike; you can't imagine comfortably inviting him to the American club. Robert Kohls writes,

Every post or American enclave has a number of people who have not been able to adjust to the country and who sit around waiting for the next boatload of American greenhorns to arrive so they can indoctrinate them on the "stupidity of the natives." You see, they have high stakes in your discontent for, if they can get you to parrot back their gripes, it proves them right.

If you need friends from home, look for veterans who have adapted well, have many local friends and can guide you as you adapt. Or, look for other novices who are willing to go daringly far into the local culture with you. Escaping to such friends is no escape; they are rather a doorway in.

But most of the time escape is just a temporary means to survival. People struggling with the barriers of culture must escape. But we can choose our escape route making sure it keeps us close to the people we came to meet in the first place. If we have chosen our escape route well, we will survive culture fatigue with faculties intact: our curiosity, our enjoyment of new friends and new customs, our desire to be partners with a strange people.

The barriers of culture are not an incidental concern. They are crucial. When God prepared the apostle Peter to present the gospel to Cornelius, a non-Jew, the Lord chose first to confront Peter over the question of what was and what was not acceptable food. This does not, at first glance, appear to be very central, or indeed a very spiritual issue. Why did God not address the theological concept of works versus grace, rather than speaking so graphically of mere food? But food mattered, as it always matters in intercultural relations. At issue was not only whether Peter could tell Cornelius certain facts about Jesus, but whether he could eat a meal with him comfortably.

God showed Peter the gentile foods that Peter would find most repulsive. He insisted that Peter accept them. He repeated the message three times, until Peter got the point. For if Peter could not eat freely with Cornelius, he could not convert him either. Nor could he fully grasp God's plan. The same may be true for us.

We must learn to accept, as acceptable to God, things that repulse us. They may be small: waiting while inefficient people delay us, eating food we don't like, sitting patiently through long, "useless" conferences. Or the obstacles may seem great: being stared at constantly, being robbed, being cheated by customs officials. We are not called on to condone sin, but we are called on to accept and love the culture these things happened in. That is, we are to accept the people themselves, not as a group to be treated with scorn, but as God's creation.

4
Those Rich Foreigners

WILL YOU FORGIVE ME if I lead you down a false trail? It has to do with servants.

They do not widely advertise it, but most missionaries have hired help. I have never seen a missionary slide presentation which included, "And this is our cook Bobby, this is our gardener Julius, and this is our night watchman Ngugi." But in countries where labor is cheap, many missionaries could offer such portraits.

One group of student summer volunteers to Kenya simply couldn't swallow this. A missionary is someone who serves. How can a servant have servants? They asked questions but felt brushed off. The missionaries they asked had long ago accepted servants as normal, and did not show sufficient agony of conscience to placate the students.

Finally the students staged a sort of strike. They would not go any farther or do any more until someone answered them. Loud and excited dialog followed until the Kenyan cook heard them from the kitchen, gathered what it was all about, and came out. He was perplexed at the uproar. He reassured the students that they were all working together for the progress of the gospel, and that his job was to cook. I don't know that he satisfied the volunteers, but they got on with their work.

Should Servants Have Servants?

I can understand the students' reaction because I shared it and, to some extent, still do. I am an American, and my culture is egalitarian. It sticks in my throat to have someone do for me, just because I am rich and he is poor, what I am quite capable of doing for myself. I dislike the idea of servants. Where I come from, nobody has servants but the ostentatious rich. And yet, despite our qualms, most missionaries like me end up with servants.

A new missionary first notices that all the other missionaries have them. He notices that having someone else do the dishes sometimes creates a pleasant after-dinner atmosphere. If he moves into missionary housing, he may "inherit" servants, with the implication quite clearly and accurately made that if he does not want them, he will have to fire them. In any case some very nice people will probably troop to his door begging for work. It may seem exploitative to have servants, but it seems plain cruel not to have them.

A good deal said in favor of hiring helpers makes sense, too. In some places you may spend so many hours making up for the lack of modern conveniences—piped water, for instance —that you accomplish little more than survival. However noble you feel carrying your own water, it is not what you came to do. And hiring helpers provides needed jobs. You share your wealth with poor people rather than manufacturers. For instance, you can hire someone to wash your clothes in the bathtub instead of buying a machine to wash them in. You will probably save money, too, since a bathtub rarely breaks down. As a bonus, your bathtub stays sparkling clean.

But I don't think all this would have convinced me. What finally broke me down was the realization that no Kenyan thought we were noble for declining to hire helpers. It was not an issue with them. Nearly all our Kenyan friends had people they hired to help them. Only we did not. They thought we were odd, not noble. So we eventually gave up and employed some part-time help.

I have deliberately routed you on a false trail. I think that most Westerners can see, on the issue of servants, how wealth can divide the rich from the poor. We can not only see it, we can feel it. We don't want to be "that kind of people." This sensitivity explains why some missionaries become quite defensive when you raise the issue. They may be right, but they don't quite feel right.

We feel this way because servants have become such a rare mark of extreme wealth in our home countries. Hardly any Christian worker could afford them in the West. But it happens that in Kenya and many other countries they are no rarity at all. Even people who are quite poor have them. (Some dislike calling them servants, however, for the word has a colonial ring.)

Real Money Barriers
But other factors involving money do form barriers between missionaries and the people they serve. We just don't realize they are barriers because they would not be in America.

A car, for instance. While I questioned having servants, I never dreamed a car could pose problems. To an American servants are sheer luxury; a car is a birthright. But my car probably divided me from the people with whom I worked far more than two, three or even four servants would have. That doesn't mean I was wrong to have a car. It means that a car—or any commodity uncommon in your new society—is an issue to be considered with care.

My car made me more effective and speeded my work. In societies where transportation is difficult, a car gives you the power to get things done. You can carry teams of evangelists, take people to the hospital, gather friends for a Bible study, travel to a remote church to speak. You save huge amounts of time and energy.

But something else happens while you are saving time: you pass by friends and coworkers who are walking or waiting for a bus. Perhaps if you spot them, you give them a lift. Perhaps you arrange to give them a lift every day. But the car remains your property, not theirs. You have the power to decide where to go and when. That usually means saying no to people as well as yes. If you give rides to everyone everywhere they want to go, you will soon find that the time and energy you saved with a car goes into transporting people. You did not become a missionary in order to drive a taxi.

So you compromise at some level. Sometimes you give rides and sometimes you do not. When you say no, you create a small gap between yourself and those you refuse. And when you say yes, you create another, different kind of gap: the gap between the giver and the receiver. If giving goes only one direction, it can create resentment.

Most missionaries come from a middle-class background. We have never thought of ourselves as rich. In becoming missionaries we may give up quite a lot and actually consider ourselves poor. But in most societies we work in, we are rich. What we consider necessities—a car, a stereo or nice dishes— may be dreams out of reach to those we work with. It may strain our imaginations to picture ourselves as the wealthy, living in splendid mansions; to our American peers we look like poor relations living in a barely adequate apartment. But Third World people may, and probably will, see us as virtual millionaires.

Emi Gichinga, a Kenyan, writes, "Westerners represent money. Even the poorest of them are considered rich. (Even if they look poor!) This stereotype dies hard."

Another Kenyan friend and I were once discussing the early Scottish missionaries to his people when he volunteered this thought: "You can tell what kind of Christians they were by looking at the kind of houses they lived in, compared to the houses they built for their African assistants." His negative reaction may not be just. But it shows the way money divides. You don't easily feel kinship with those wealthier than you.

Paul Buttrey relates a telling story from Taiwan:

A missionary had spent his first two years in language school. During that time he had participated in the services of a local Chinese church of his denomination. At the end of the two years, he went to the pastor, telling him that he was now ready to begin his ministry of evangelism and church planting. He felt he needed a Chinese coworker. He asked the pastor if he could recommend anyone for this work.

The pastor asked him one question: "What salary will he receive? Will he have the same standard of living as you?"

The missionary replied that he could not provide that large a salary. The pastor replied that he could not think of anyone who would be interested in such a position!

The Problem of Generosity

How do we break through this barrier? Generosity is probably the first impulse for most missionaries. They may not see a way to pay a coworker at an American standard, but at least they try to pay him better than his local peers. Missionaries may give out loans to new friends, shower beggars with coins or double the cook's salary.

But these acts of generosity often backfire. The coworker gets used to living at a higher standard, and eventually cannot think of working for the local church—they could not pay him. Those who take loans have difficulty repaying them, and rather than becoming closer friends, they deliberately stay away because they feel the weight of the obligation. Generosity may, rather than breaking down the barrier of money, increase it, by increasing the dependence of others on us. Missionaries become more than wealthy. They become lords with serfs.

I traveled once to a remote desert area with a team of Kenyans involved in church agricultural projects. They complained bitterly against the missionaries in the area. They said missionaries practically bribed people with money and materials. They had big vehicles. They paid evangelists and pastoral helpers. They bought musical instruments. They gave food in hungry times. So the Kenyans I was with said, "When the church wants to send a Kenyan pastor, these people say, 'We don't want him! We want the missionary!' Missionaries have ensured they can never be replaced."

I am sure the missionaries never dreamed of this reaction. They were simply doing all they could to help in the most generous way they knew. But their very goodheartedness had created a problem.

You can mitigate this reaction by being careful how you give. Instead of dispensing handouts personally, you can give through local, self-sustaining structures. However, such careful giving takes time. In place of giving out food, for instance, you would want to arrange for instruction in agricultural techniques. But at some time you have to choose priorities. Teaching agriculture takes more time than giving out food, and if your priority is church planting you may have little time left over. But can you withhold your gifts because you do not have the time to give properly? Do you refuse the hungry person food because feeding him may increase dependency? Most missionaries choose to give, even if they know handouts are not the answer in the long run. They become to some extent pipelines, valued (or resented) for how much they give rather than for who they are.

To avoid that, some choose another route: they live on a stipend, so that they have no more than the people they work with. Overseas Missionary Fellowship, for instance, asks its missionaries to live on the salary a local high-school teacher would earn. They are thus not rich, though they may still earn more than local pastors or illiterate peasants. Some missionaries go considerably further, trying to live at a level of genuine poverty in the culture they serve.

Everyone agrees that modest living is desirable. The huge missionary houses of an earlier era are now rare. But the question is, what constitutes modesty? Who defines it? And how far should we go? To go "all the way" appeals to many people of my generation. It requires great sacrifice. It suits our antimaterialistic feelings.

I think those who have tried going "all the way" will admit, however, that the results are less spectacular than might be hoped. You do not automatically win acceptance because of your sacrifices. You may even win resentment or suspicion, not just from fellow missionaries (who will certainly sniff at you), but from the very people you sought to identify with.

In the '60s and '70s a good many hippies visited Africa, no doubt expecting to be liked and admired for their simple living. They must have been surprised at their reception. To this day Africans remember them with disgust and horror. They would plainly have preferred the company of loud, rich American tourists in plaid pants.

For one thing, the hippies used drugs and were sexually immoral. But the resentment had a deeper basis: Africans saw the hippies were play-acting. They were not really poor. They were pretending to be poor. This insulted African values; though poor, almost any African would like to be rich. Most Africans see wealth as a sign of blessing. So do many people who have not had our opportunities to overindulge ourselves.

So nationals will not necessarily respect a missionary who chooses to live simply. Simplicity for simplicity's sake? That has no appeal. And if they think a missionary is living in poverty just to be like them, they may feel patronized. They would not like that any more than a child likes an adult who talks down to him.

There is an advantage to simple living, however. The advantage lies not in some moral virtue inherent in depriving yourself. The advantage is that you become less alien to those you serve. You share their problems. They find it easier to relate to someone who lives by a familiar pattern more or less at their level.

We remain, in truth, rich. Even if we limit our income, we know where more money can be found, and that profoundly affects our approach to problems. We fly on silver airplanes to and from a rich land; those we serve know that the land we come from is wealthy, regardless of what they see us wear or eat. Must we try to eradicate even these signs of our wealth? Should we give up flying home for furloughs? Disguise our nationality? This would not be wise even if it were possible.

We cannot help being rich in comparison to the people we serve. Much of our effectiveness, if the truth be told, flows from our riches. In simplest terms a missionary is a person with a message. But the missionary cannot stop being what and who he is. His background, education, organizational skills, language ability and money are mixed in inextricably with his personality and gifts. I cannot truthfully echo Peter, "Silver and gold have I none." At times I wish I could; it would certainly simplify matters, eliminating the barrier of money at one stroke. On the other hand, I could not have started a magazine in Kenya without lots and lots of silver and gold.

Then how exactly should we live? "Modestly" is not precise enough to answer particular questions; a dozen mission boards will define "modest living" in a dozen ways. We do not want to be lords living above those we serve, separated from them. But if we try to live strictly at their level, we usually reduce our efficiency—we miss our cars, our household conveniences. And, in any case, they still see us as rich—which we are. There is no exact formula for living "properly"; and failing to find a formula, many missionaries shrug their shoulders and live in a way they find comfortable. They continue to agonize over the problem. But if you ask them why they choose to live the way they do, they do not have a clear answer.

In Search of a Formula

In the last decade, Christians in America and Europe have expended considerable energy trying to find a formula for the "proper" way to live in their affluent societies. Two extremes dominate the intellectual arena, with quite a lot of muddle in between. One school emphasizes that wealth is God's blessing: if you want to find godly living, you should look first among the rich, whom God has blessed. The opposing school claims that God dwells mainly with the poor, as their protector, and if you want to know God you will have to join him there. The first school suggests that you live as a "king's kid," assuming the privileges of wealth. The second school suggests you sell all, give to the poor and live communally.

Temperamentally I lean toward the latter view, probably because I graduated from high school in 1968. But my time in Africa made me think both schools wrong. Both make the characteristically Western error of overvaluing money. I mean to say not only that money dominates the thinking of conservative capitalists, but that it equally dominates the thinking of left-leaning liberals. Marxism, as I see it, is little more than a reaction to the ideology of capitalism; it thinks in the same heartlessly materialistic way. Its nightmares and its utopia resemble those that capitalists dream; they are totally materialistic. We have all been infected with such thinking, for it thoroughly infects the Western world. And it can easily infect our view of missionary work.

I went to Africa expecting that living at close proximity to poverty would increase my awareness of (and guilt about) others' poverty. Statistically, Africa is by far the poorest continent. I expected poverty to overwhelm me, and I welcomed the prospect of a changed attitude. My attitude did in fact change, but not exactly as I had expected.

I certainly found poor people. Whatever goes by the name of poverty in America is wealthy by comparison. I saw pastors who could hardly study the Bible because they had worked all day and at night had no private, quiet spot in their small house with their large family. I became friends with people who could not afford to indulge themselves even in an egg; they survived on corn meal, and all the goods they saw in shop windows were absolutely impossible for them. I knew husbands separated from their wives for months at a time because the husband had left his rural home to find work in the city, but did not earn enough to support his family there. Poverty is a mean and endless burden, especially in the city beside so many who have so much.

But I also saw, paradoxically, the generosity of poor people. We stayed with rural families who had next to nothing; eking a living from a tiny two-acre farm, they probably didn't see $100 a year. Yet when we left they piled our little car with gifts; every available inch was filled with fruits and vegetables and meat and whatever they had. We had tried to be generous to them, but they always outgave us—with gusto. It was embarrassing to take from people who had so little. Yet clearly it gave them joy to give to us, and we could not refuse. They seemed to have forgotten they were supposed to be miserable. They did not even seem to know how poor they were, or how rich we were by comparison.

Preaching to a Starving Man
I have often heard that you can't preach the gospel to a man who is starving. This saying paints a vivid picture of a well-fed missionary rising from a sumptuous meal to deliver a Bible-thumping message of salvation to someone about to expire from hunger. The picture is so vivid it can dazzle us, so we accept propositions that are simply not true.

The picture could imply, for instance, that a starving man is disinterested in spiritual things—that only after he has eaten can you interest him in eternal life. It is true that you or I could not interest him in eternal life. But what if you found two starving men side by side in a truly hopeless situation, one a Christian and one not? What would they talk of? I suspect they would talk of eternal life. Few people are so interested in the hereafter as those who are about to enter it.

Spiritual life is not a luxury, of concern only to those who have more "basic" needs filled. It is the most basic need. People say that prostitution is the world's oldest profession, but I suspect it is more probably the priesthood. Nearly any culture, ancient or modern, poor or wealthy, has a religion they cling to tenaciously. The hunger for meaning, and for God, is virtually universal.

So how is the statement "You can't preach to a starving man" true? It is true in that you can rarely interest someone in a gospel of love if you yourself do not show love. Your own faith would be inauthentic. James wrote, "Suppose a brother or sister is without clothes and daily food. If one of you says to him, 'Go, I wish you well; keep warm and well fed,' but does nothing about his physical needs, what good is it? In the same way, faith by itself, if it is not accompanied by action, is dead" (Jas 2:15-17).

This says you cannot be genuinely Christian while ignoring issues of food and clothing. But it does not say that to have a relationship you must first eliminate any differences in income. It does not suggest that the rich and the poor are naturally, inevitably, alienated.

One of the chief lessons I got from poor Kenyans is that life is more than money, and that relationships are not dependent on income levels. I became friends with them, and they accepted me as I am. I could not stop being wealthy or bring them to my level. I could only try to be generous in what amounted to insignificant ways—ways that did not alter the fundamental realities of rich and poor. Yet they humbled me by joyfully accepting my friendship.

Once we see this point, we can quit worrying so much about an exact formula for "modest living." If other things matter more than money, our thoughts naturally turn to asking how money can lift or destroy these more important things. Money becomes relative, a resource to be used. That, of course, is what Jesus' parable of the talents ought to lead us to. The point is not how much each servant receives—that question is virtually irrelevant—but how each uses it for his master's welfare.

A Case of Begging from Beggars

Bedan Mbugua, a Kenyan, tells a story about a research project he did among the Turkana people. I have mused on the story quite often, and I believe it has helped me understand how to treat our money.

The Turkana live in northern Kenya, a wild and desolate desert region. They are notorious beggars. They are also terribly poor, and in times of drought many starve to death. But in poverty or plenty, they remain beggars. It is part of their culture, evidently, to ask for anything and everything. The few Westerners who live with them, mostly missionaries, find this discouraging. If you say yes to one Turkana, ten stand at your door the next day. You cannot disentangle yourself from an endless series of requests except by saying no each time. But that solution is uncomfortable, since the needs are obvious and missionaries have incredible riches in comparison to the Turkana. A few missionaries have tried giving without reservation and have become mere conduits for goods. You cannot accomplish much else when a seemingly endless stream of people come to your door asking for food. The Turkana are not embarrassed to go on asking. One imagines them at heaven's gate, trying to cadge a shilling from St. Peter.

Bedan tried a slightly different approach. He gave food freely to anyone who asked until he had given everything away. Then, instead of going to buy more, he went to some of the Turkana people and begged food from them. They happily shared. He came to the conclusion that begging is, among other things, a means for the Turkana to get acquainted. They beg from each other. Asking for something is like saying "How are you?" When Bedan acted to them in kind, relationships began to open. They stopped seeing him as a conduit for goods and began to see him as a peer.

This gives a flash of insight, but we must be careful not to let it blind us. We might take his story to mean that we should live in complete poverty. But Bedan did not do that. He had not stopped being rich. He had a Land Rover. Since he had money, he could buy more food. The Turkana are not fools, and they must have known this. But in their society he had made an essentially friendly gesture. By begging from them he had found a way to put aside his differentness in favor of the sociability that binds all people together.

We are social animals, however variously we express it. One of the discoveries I most enjoyed in Kenya was that, under our cultural differences, personality types often stay the same. I found the gabby neighbor, the lonely widow, the jolly, booming shopkeeper, the stumbling, inarticulate wise man, and so on. We need to get on this level of personality, leaving cultural stereotypes behind. Bedan, by begging back from the Turkana, found a way to break through to it. But the way he broke through would not be the same in another culture.

His story doesn't give me, then, a detailed plan for action. But it gives a principle for making plans, a goal that makes use of money but doesn't set a certain lifestyle or income level as the norm. Our goal, I believe, should be to break down social barriers. Any use of money that brings us closer to the people we serve is good. Any use that separates us is bad.

Using Money to Bring People Together

I don't say using money to create sociability is the only worthwhile goal. Money can feed and clothe people; it makes a medium for compassion. But when in helping people you end up distancing yourself from them, I have my doubts about the long-term effectiveness of the help. Cold, depersonalized help usually demeans the person who receives, and breeds dependency. If we keep in the front of our minds that we want to come closer to people, I believe our giving will prove effective in alleviating poverty as well.

If you buy a car, you will find many uses for it that facilitate socializing. You can use it to gather people for trips, to bring them to your home, to travel to theirs. But it can also be a barrier. A car will keep you off buses and trains, where you could meet your neighbors and share a daily experience which people chat and sympathize with each other about. A car also creates the barrier of the giver and the receiver: you resent being "used," and they resent having to ask for help and putting themselves at your mercy.

If you have a good stereo, it may attract neighbors to your house to listen to records. It may, on the other hand, highlight your differentness if you do not have any records they like. They may irritate you if they scratch your records, and if your irritation shows they may never forgive you for it.

In most cultures, one of the most important decisions you make is where to live. Location is related, of course, to price and style, but how much you have to pay is not the chief issue. The question is whether the location helps people feel free to visit you or puts them off. Ideally, your home should be easy to get to. Public transportation should pass nearby. It should be easy to find. If the neighborhood is unfamiliar to would-be friends, they will be less likely to follow your directions, however clear, to find it. Huge gates, barking dogs and high walls do not invite people in—and they are standard equipment for the upper class in many countries, because burglary is so common. Mission compounds are rarely inviting, either. They often have a different ambiance than the world outside; what feels restful to you may seem alien to your would-be friend.

Many of these indications suggest living more simply, or in a poorer neighborhood than you would by instinct. But not all. It may be good to buy space—space for people to feel comfortable in, extra rooms for people to sleep in. It may be good, for the same reason, to buy comfortable furniture.

I realize this criterion—sociability—will not satisfy everyone, particularly because it doesn't tell you whether wealth is good or bad, or what exact standard you should live at. It doesn't leave you totally up in the air, though. It gives a decisive test that will push you in a certain direction. If you inherit a big mission house, it will make you think about how the house can be used to welcome people. If you own a stereo, it will make you buy some records that appeal to your would-be friends. If you have a car, it will make you think of using it to visit people instead of sights. Subtly but surely it will push you toward people. One by one the barriers money causes will be identified and surmounted.

You will find this easier to do if you don't bring too many things with you. Historically missionaries sailed with many "missionary barrels" of possessions, and today most missionaries ship in large crates of goods. In some situations these possessions are necessary, but it is wise to be cautious. After all, people survive in the country you are going to, and in nearly every country on earth there are rich people as well as poor. You can buy the things you need locally most of the time, although the price, because of import restrictions, may be high. But if you bring them with you in a crate, you will have decided what you should have before you arrive. You will have a huge American refrigerator instead of the small one most people around the world use. You will have nice dishes instead of the cheaper kind made locally. I believe it is best to start with a few precious things that make home "home," and build up more after you have studied the situation. This may cost more, but the choice is worth the money. It is psychologically difficult to "build down" from a vast store of possessions you brought with you.

What about Work?
I have so far concentrated on social life, that is, on what happens *after* work. That is my main focus in this book. But we cannot draw a neat line dividing social life from work, and I want to sketch a few remarks about the way money affects work. Here, too, it can divide you from the people you serve.

Paul carried money from the newly planted churches back to church headquarters in Jerusalem. I don't think there is any evidence of money going in the opposite direction. In our time money flows exclusively in that opposite direction, toward the newer churches, to support missionaries and often to support the new churches' programs.

You expect to support a brand new church financially, for a limited time. And where no church yet exists, a missionary can't very well take up a collection. However, large sums of money are still flowing to churches that have been established for generations. Mission money seems like an addictive drug. It's hard to foresee, ever, a situation like Paul's where the newer churches take up a collection for the old. Why is it so? Why, after many decades, are churches not self-supporting?

A fundamental reason is that few Christians in the Third World give large percentages of their income to the church. Of course, they are often poor. But they probably are no poorer than the people of the Bible who gave at least ten per cent of their income to the Temple. It is a simple rule that if ten families tithe, they can support a pastor or a missionary at their own standard of living. But such giving is, I believe, quite rare.

Why is this so? It is not that people are ungenerous. Most Third World cultures, living nearer to rural life, maintain a strong emphasis on hospitality. You will see tremendous generosity when they feed you the last food in the house, even while they know that you are not in need as they are. They support unemployed relatives for years at a time.

But they give less generously to the institutional church, and so money is the root of all kinds of evil within the church. Not enough is given to support enough pastors; the lack of good, educated pastors drives young people away from the church; and since these educated young earn the most money, the church remains poor. Money may be misappropriated; my own church in Kenya lost large sums on several different occasions while I was there. That hardly encouraged more generous giving. And from my point of view the churches often raise money for the wrong things: to build a large stone cathedral, for instance, while pastors literally go hungry.

Sometimes missionaries take blame for poor giving. "They did not teach people to give," some say. But I doubt whether this is the main explanation. I blame history. We are heirs of a church which grew up under the European period of colonization. This spread of empire coincided with a huge leap of material prosperity in the Western world through industrialization. Colonizers went everywhere, and the church went with them. Some have called missionaries the vanguard of colonial imperialism. The missionary went first, they say, and the trader soon followed. David Livingstone's influential writings to the effect that Christianity would only spread in Africa along with commerce, which would break down traditional social structures, have encouraged this belief.

I suspect, however, that any link between Christianity and commerce was largely unintentional and even unconscious. Some missionaries actually opposed the colonial commercial order. But whatever they said or thought, missionaries could not escape the fact that they came bringing a Christianity laden with gifts: hospitals, schools, farming materials, little stone churches.

And Christianity came side by side with the riches of industrial society: metal pipe for plumbing and sewage, formulas for building roads, cars and trucks to ride on them, steel for bridges, kerosene and later electricity for light. Even if the missionary saw he needed to teach giving, how could he? What sense would it make to ask people to bring gifts to the church? For what purpose? The missionaries apparently possessed the wealth of the world and were giving it out. Should their flock bring them more? Probably giving to the church must always be taught. Giving is not a natural impulse, or the New Testament letters would not need to remind people of it as often as they do. But Paul preached to people who were rich compared to his peers in Jerusalem. The fact that the gospel in our time came from the rich to the poor short-circuited teaching about giving.

St. Paul Built No Hospitals

And of course the missionaries stayed, perhaps too long. The contrast between this and Paul's missionary journeys, in which he usually left a church to struggle for itself after a matter of months, has often been noted. Fewer commentators have noted that Paul's situation was different. Because he took his message from a backwater to the center of the world, he had only the gospel itself to carry. Jerusalem's health care was not superior to Rome's, so he did not build hospitals. Christians in Corinth read Greek as well as Christians in Antioch, so he had no need to build schools and staff them. He might be as compassionate as anyone could imagine but feel no duty to launch a single institution or build a single building. He had only good news, which is extremely portable and can be conveyed to an educated person in a matter of weeks.

The missionaries of our time, however, could not ignore starvation, disease or illiteracy, for they had the means to do away with them. To do so they founded institutions, which do not grow up in a day or a year. To this day missionaries represent money and skills to run these institutions; the newer churches remain weak in these. So missionaries prolong their stay—and their giving.

Nobody likes this situation. But how do we get out of it? As both national churches and missions take the problem more seriously, financial independence is slowly coming to the churches of the Third World. But most have a long way to go.

Most new missionaries will have little say in mission or church policy to speed this independence. Nor will they often put their hands on large sums of money for distribution. Large-scale relief and development projects are now mostly out of the hands of mission organizations. They belong to new groups, such as World Vision, which usually hesitate to call themselves missionaries.

But most missionaries, whatever their work, will find needs and requests for money. Someone doing church planting may find that his newly founded church would like to have a build-

ing to meet in—even if they do not live in buildings themselves. Someone doing youth evangelism will find a lively interest in music and conclude that electric guitars, drums,
amplifiers and speakers would be useful. Someone training
lay leaders in Bible study may find one young man keen and
capable to join the work—but the church lacks the vision or
means (often the two go together) to pay him. A doctor working in a mobile clinic finds that many of his patients have a
protein deficiency which might be cured if only the cows
were of a better grade and gave more milk. A Bible-college
teacher learns by accident that the head of the church has
drawn plans to build a large chapel at the school—and then
the head of the church comes to ask whether he will help raise
funds to build it. It is not easy, or necessarily wise, to say a flat
no to these and other needs and requests. Like it or not,
money has done much to aid the spread of the good news. In
any case, we are who we are: wealthy people. How can we refuse help which we are capable of giving?

My own belief is that aid, whether given to children through
World Vision or in the form of technology transfers through
the United Nations, is not nearly so effective as is widely believed. The reason? Lack of money and expertise is rarely the
crucial obstacle to economic development. Human attitudes,
of the oppressors and of the oppressed, keep people poor,
and they are not easy to change. Certainly money doesn't
change them. It can even make them worse.

Yet I believe in, and give to, aid projects. In my own work in
Kenya, I oversaw the transfer of about $100,000 to start a
magazine. I would do it no differently. Not only does money
help, but giving is a normal part of any good human relationship. It may not do all that people expect from it. But that is
not a good enough reason to stop giving. We give because we
are human beings, and a gift emphasizes our care for each
other.

So if the church wants to build a cathedral, I will without
grudging do my share to see it built. If a singing group wants

an amplifier, I will consider whether it lies in my power and responsibility to make them happy. If people come to my door hungry, I will give them food. What all the long-term effects of these actions may be, I am not sure.

Do I not give responsibly, then? I try to show my responsibility by not forgetting other long-term effects I am more sure of. I try to see that through my giving friendships develop, that the church extends its vision and that the people involved become stronger in character. I guard particularly against building dependency, which is deadly to the person and our relationship.

Focusing on People

Whether you give food for the hungry or amplifiers for teenagers, it is a temporal gift, not eternal. Money buys buildings, starts programs, pays salaries, feeds people. Only indirectly does it build up people. Yet people are the only "long-term" projects we know about, for they alone are eternal. All the rest will vanish, will rot or rust or break down or become outmoded, or will burn up in the final judgment. Only people will endure.

So when I give, I keep my eye on the people involved. I want them to grow because of my generosity, not shrink. Gifts may encourage or discourage growth in many different and unpredictable ways. A guitar amplifier in one sense may retard a musician's development, by encouraging him to make music that is too Westernized for his setting. It may make him dependent on me, rather than his own people and his own wits. But it may also give him experience, the chance to make mistakes, and the confidence that comes from being trusted.

The first time that money became a divisive issue in the New Testament, the Grecian Jews in Jerusalem felt they were being neglected in the distribution of aid (Acts 6:1-7). They publicly complained. The apostles' solution was to appoint seven men to oversee food distribution. Judging from their names, all seven were Grecian Jews—even though all the apostles were Galileans, a quite separate ethnic group.

Why choose only Grecian Jews? It could be that Grecian Jews were inherently superior in money matters. But more likely it had to do with trust. The apostles wanted to bend over backward to make certain that, by generously trusting them, suspicion could be ended. The issue for them was not just the efficiency of food distribution. The issue involved human feelings, questions of trust.

Dealing with money by focusing on people, not efficiency, is an art form; it is not a science. You cannot make a formula for deciding whether to provide a guitar amplifier, because the gift involves relationships: relationships between people, relationships between one culture and another, relationships between God and his people. But this kind of giving should not seem strange to us. We decide on gifts in exactly this way each Christmas. How do you decide what to give, and how much to spend? You try to give useful gifts, but primarily you give to fit the person and to strengthen the bonds of friendship.

When I prepare to give, I pray that God will make me sensitive to the people involved. I meditate on their needs, spiritual and psychological as well as material. I ask other people for ideas. When I give, the gift goes with a prayer it will help and not hinder the person who receives it, and that it will strengthen his or her free friendship with me.

5
At Home with the Language

I AM A POOR ONE to write about the barrier of language, for I have yet to master a second one. I speak French poorly and Kiswahili hardly at all. Only my intentions are good. But if I am not a model, perhaps I am a specimen.

Of course, there are plenty of missionaries who become really good at languages. I envy them; they have overcome a major barrier, perhaps *the* major barrier between cultures. But in talking to them I have not discovered any special secret. They just say what you would expect: "practice, practice, practice."

So perhaps as a specimen of failure I may be helpful. It is always easier to explain why a car breaks down than why it works well. Since by no means all missionaries become fluent in their hosts' language—in fact, real fluency may be more the exception than the rule—I hope something can be gained by analyzing why the machine broke down. Then perhaps we can fix it, or maintain it better.

The embarrassing thing is that the people we go to are so good at languages. At least they are in Kenya. In Nairobi you can easily hear a dozen languages on the street in a matter of five minutes. The ordinary high-school student speaks at least three well. Their facility makes it difficult for you to gain facility. Often they speak English and are eager to use it with you. (As they improve their English, their status and potential earnings improve.)

The British have long been under the impression that anyone, no matter how thick, can understand an English sentence if it is repeated loudly and impatiently. Americans start a step farther behind. We find it difficult to believe that there is any language other than English, except as a high-school subject like trigonometry, invented apparently just to harass people. I remember arriving in France as a student. My American roommate returned from a tour of the streets and said, "These people must be really smart. Even the little kids know French." He was joking, of course, but we did find it startling to see a whole nation living day after day without English.

I had lived in Nairobi for some time before I began to see that a person's mother tongue mattered to him. I just felt lucky to land in a place where English was an official language. I was assured at the beginning that I did not need to learn Kiswahili or any other language for my work, and the information was quite correct. Not only could I produce a magazine in English, but English was the only suitable language for it. Since by fortune Kenyans had already learned my language, I was not inconvenienced by the need to learn theirs. And indeed, this was to my advantage. It meant I could accomplish something in my work right off, while others spent years mastering the elements of a difficult language like Chinese.

But, as I have already stressed, being a missionary is more than doing work. If you put any emphasis on social life, a mother tongue immediately seems more important.

Play a mental game with me. Try to think of the South without its accent. Drive through Alabama and Mississippi and imagine people speaking to you in the colorless accent of network TV. Nobody says, "Sho' nuff!" or "Y'all come down." They speak "normally." What have you done? You have taken the South out of the South. It has become a Disneyland plaza of *Gone with the Wind:* the sights are Southern, but the attendants come in the gate to work every morning. Stripping the South of its language, you strip it of its personality.

The same is true, only more so, of other countries and cultures. More than bare communication is at stake. They themselves live in their languages. Until you know the rhythms and inflections of speech, the untranslatable jokes made when someone twists a language's tail, you do not fully know the people speaking. Language carries many meanings behind the dictionary definitions of the words. This is particularly so of a mother tongue, or regional dialect. An individual may actually have learned to speak a second language better. For instance, since Kikuyu contains no scientific and few business terms, few high-level Kikuyu people would try to conduct business without English. But Kikuyu remains the language their mothers spoke to them. It is the language of home, the language of memory and the language of rest.

My wife and I had the privilege of joining a church fellowship group whose members, mostly older than ourselves, held top responsibilities in the Kenyan government. They spoke impeccable English at work all day. They used English at church, and because of our presence they spoke English at our fellowship group. Most days they spoke far more English than Kikuyu, I suspect. But we noticed that as the fellowship went late, and fatigue and relaxation set in, they lapsed more and more into Kikuyu. They would realize we didn't understand, explain what they had said—and then lapse into Kikuyu again.

It tires you out to speak a second language, no matter how well you do it. It tires our hosts to talk to us. It tires us to try to use their language. The fatigue urges us to separate, to do our work, and then to relax, speaking our own language, at home. Language thus keeps us apart even when we can communicate well in a common language like English. But when a foreigner speaks a local language, he is deeply and thankfully welcomed in.

The Language of Love

What you don't know about, you don't miss. Because I could communicate in English with nearly any of my friends and coworkers, I didn't experience frustration in not knowing Kiswahili or another African language well. But drifting on the edge of my memory are a few occasions which showed me that, without more language, I missed a dimension of friendship.

I had come to help start a magazine. I remember one day when the staff began discussing love and language over lunch. Hannah, the office secretary, claimed that you could not say "I love you" in her mother language of Kikuyu. Hannah is a romantic sort of person, and she shivered and said, "Oh, when my husband says, 'I love you,' I feel BZZZZ." Bedan immediately challenged her. He gave Kikuyu words that could express "I love you," and he asserted strongly that those would have more meaning than the English. To an African, he said, an English "I love you" would have a superficial, childish subtext.

They argued for quite a long time, with others joining in. Hannah would not give up. If her husband said "I love you" in their mother tongue, she said, "I would never feel BZZZZ. I want to hear it in English." To her the Western concept of romantic love went with English. Some of the others agreed. Love in English seemed different from love in their language. Of course, I could not really follow the discussion or understand the differences because I spoke only English.

We regularly ate lunch together at a kiosk, an open-air stall made of cardboard and plastic where a stew of beans and corn was served. I was frequently lost in discussions. A lot of the humor not only had a different pace but took as its text the differences in accent and language between the several dozen tribes of Kenya. Many of the jokes required a knowledge of not just Kiswahili, but Kiswahili as spoken by an uneducated person. Probably because Kenya is so polyglot, language took great prominence in humor.

But what is life without humor? And particularly, what is social life without humor? And how can there be full-hearted humor in an alien language? Here I find the most unanswerable argument in favor of learning the mother tongue of the people we serve, and learning it well: we ought to laugh with them. However impossible that seems at first—for humor is almost always the subtlest use of language—we ought to aim for it.

Of course, if I had never eaten in that kiosk, I would not have heard those jokes. Had I stuck to my work and kept my own separate social life, I would never have felt the deficiencies of speaking English. But then, though I did my job "well," I would not have succeeded. Perhaps I could have put out a creditable magazine, but it would never have had that African "feel" that made it click, that made the circulation grow, that made the staff excited and willing to sacrifice to see it succeed. I am glad I ate in the kiosk. I wonder how much better work might have gone had I learned fluent Kiswahili as well.

When the Holy Spirit broke through at Pentecost, he spoke to men and women in their mother tongues, though they probably knew at least one and possibly two common languages. But Greek or Aramaic would not have provoked the same heartfelt response.

A crowd came together in bewilderment, because each one heard them speaking in his own language. Utterly amazed, they asked: "Are not all these men who are speaking Galileans? Then how is it that each of us hears them in his own native language? Parthians, Medes and Elamites; residents of Mesopotamia, Judea and Cappadocia, Pontus and Asia, Phrygia and Pamphylia, Egypt and the parts of Libya near

Cyrene; visitors from Rome (both Jews and converts to Judaism); Cretans and Arabs—we hear them declaring the wonders of God in our own tongues!" Amazed and perplexed, they asked one another, "What does this mean?" (Acts 2:6-12)

Such startling and powerfully spiritual communication ought to be our goal.

A "Do-able" Task

What keeps us from learning languages? One would think that all missionaries would succeed at language learning, for few missionary goals are so "do-able." Of course, some find languages more difficult than others do, but languages are beyond no person of normal intelligence. If you learned one language, your brain can accommodate two. Indeed, when someone is thrown into a situation where he has to learn another language or starve, he always learns it—just as the American immigrants did. If you plan to plant five churches, or reach one tribe with the gospel, or develop twenty competent Bible teachers, you may not be sure of success. But if you plan to learn a language, you can most certainly succeed. It is within your reach.

And to aid you, most missions have established language schools, elaborate and expensive facilities which make it their business to help you learn. Over the past twenty years a great deal of educational research has vastly improved the teaching techniques of these schools, and most have expensive audio equipment which greatly speeds the language-learning process.

Of course, language schools only teach major languages, not small tribal tongues, simply because there would not be enough interest in the latter to justify a school. But Thomas and Elizabeth Brewster's LAMP (Language Acquisition Made Practical) techniques have spread widely as a way to learn a language without a school. They emphasize learning simply by following systematic personal contacts in your new home.

The Brewsters claim it works faster and more effectively than language school does. "If you set out to learn a language you will possibly fail," Brewster says. "But if you set out to have deep relationships with people, you will learn their language."

Yet with all these resources to accomplish a "do-able" task, many missionaries still fail to learn a language really well. This is so not only where English is widespread. In every part of the world missionaries "get by" with a modest facility. They speak with atrocious, grating accents. They make mistakes. They use a "lingua franca" when the people they serve know it as only a second language. For instance, they work with South American Indian tribes using Spanish as the medium of communication.

What keeps us so backward? The first barrier is, of course, our preference not to be tortured. You cannot learn a language apart from suffering. Some languages are harder than others, but no language is easy. Total immersion is the fastest way to learn, immersion for stretches of time as long as you can stomach. Hardly anything will more certainly produce depression and anger. You are deprived of your speech, which is worse than losing a leg. The temptation to quit early, to call the process complete and go back to being whole, is very, very strong.

A second factor is pride. None of us likes being made a fool of in public; we fear making mistakes and only volunteer for projects where we can look reasonably competent. You can't learn a language this way. You *will* make mistakes; you *will* say stupid things; people *will* laugh at your incompetence. You learn a language as you learn to swim: by flailing around. The "missionary mentality," of great and inspired Christians coming to help needy people, does not fit with the reality of being snickered at by a congregation of the "needy." So some missionaries speak through translators ("until I get the local lingo") or simply stay out of situations where they have to expose themselves. But they never learn that way.

A third factor is the politeness of our hosts. Consider, if

you will, all the patience and pity lavished on a foreigner who comes to the United States without knowing English. Our compassion would not fill an eyedropper. Foreign students in the United States persistently complain that Americans greet everything they say with "What?" We soon take out of them any vanity they feel for how well they know English. In many cultures such bluntness is rude.

Our Third World hosts, in contrast, generally coddle us into thinking we speak their language admirably, if we speak it at all. I don't know how many times I was told that I speak Kiswahili like a native, when the plain truth is that I have to think to say how many oranges I want. I would have been better off had people said to me, "What? You don't speak Kiswahili yet?" But they didn't.

Becoming a Baby

Children learn languages fast, I suspect because they have so little to say. Their highest priority is play, and they need few words to kick balls or climb trees with their peers. They do not mind making mistakes with words, because words mean so little to them. But the more you are grown and entangled in friendships and family, the more of yourself you must sacrifice in the process of learning a language. You are less flexible when you have deeper roots.

Family responsibilities complicate adults' learning. Husbands and wives may try to use a foreign language with each other, but they rarely keep it up. An adult who loses the use of language becomes a baby, stripped of capability and dignity. You cannot tolerate such indignity for long within your own family, where communication and mutual reassurance are too urgent to be played at.

As a result, married couples will learn more slowly, for they will be less immersed in the language. Families with small children face special difficulties. The wife often must care for the children and so has little time to practice the new language. Her husband does, and he soon improves. This discrepancy makes it all the more difficult for them to work together at language learning. The woman, who came with the intention of sharing in ministry, may feel isolated and frustrated. Of course, as her husband then needs to spend more time with her—and speaking English, not some foreign tongue—his own learning is retarded. Hiring a maid, or living with a local family may alleviate this problem, for then the local language becomes part of the home. But these solutions offer their own unique strains. Inevitably, single people can learn languages fastest and best. Perhaps we need to rethink 1 Corinthians 7:32-35—on the advantages of single living—in the context of missions.

Perhaps the greatest barrier to learning a language well is impatience. You were not called as a missionary, you think, in order to learn a language. The language is a nuisance (cultural pride lies hidden here) that must be dealt with so that you can get on with more important things.

At the time of this writing, Paul and Mary Jeanne Buttrey in Taiwan tell me their church youth group has asked them to speak several times. Most of the time they have said no, because they don't think they know the language well enough. They could be out speaking in translation every weekend, they say, but they have chosen not to for the same reason. Their patience is admirable after two years of language study. But how long will they last? At some point they must get involved, even though they are not yet perfect in language. They never will be perfect.

Once you open the door to work, however, more floods in than you can possibly do. You become too busy to study the language. My grandfather did not learn Urdu perfectly in over thirty years largely because he was pulled out of language training to put up buildings. You rarely learn a language by putting up buildings; you may learn a pidgin version that communicates facts but not nuances. (You may, conversely, learn something of real people that you will never learn in language school. My grandfather, by all accounts, had great rapport.)

To learn a language well, you must make learning it your first and most important job for some months or even years. You will want desperately to get on to more important things. But patience will reap a great reward.

Learning a Language a Hundred Times

Perhaps, having surveyed the barriers to learning a language, I can turn now to positive motivation: the blessings.

Learning a language involves all of you, and it shapes all of you. Not only the end result—a language mastered—is worthwhile. The process itself can make you better fit for cross-cultural work. Those who understand the value of this sometimes excruciating process may stick to it better.

Learning stretches your patience, first of all. You do not learn a language once, but a hundred times. The first ninety-nine times you learn a word you forget it. When you try to remember it, your mind moves so slowly you can hear it rusting. Meanwhile, people wait eagerly for what will come out of your mouth, or disturb your concentration by offering hopeful suggestions of what you might be trying to say.

This is a close analog to any work in a foreign culture. Ignorance appears invincible; you stand in a tiny cloud of light with yards of darkness beyond. In such an environment you need not only flexibility but the tolerance for failure called patience. Learning a language is a good school for that. Some people are better at languages than others, but hardly anyone finds it easy. It takes a long time, usually at least a year, to learn any language with reasonable facility. That means for at least nine months you are the stupidest person around. You may never be better than dull in your second language.

Learning a language also teaches humility. Westerners tend to be arrogant, without knowing it. We find it difficult to accept help from the people we are supposed to be helping. They take our advice; we don't take theirs. I don't know where our hosts find the patience to listen to yet another American telling them, "What we've been learning in America is..."

But when you are learning their language, you have to daily acknowledge one field where they are clearly (compared to you) brilliant. You have to constantly ask for help and correction. The habit can grow on you. Some people learn to ask, not just what a particular word means, but what the best way to introduce a particular subject might be. They begin to listen not only to the inflections of speech but to the unspoken assumptions and approaches you learn from no books.

Humility need not mean sadness and contrition. A better humility is dressed in enthusiasm. Marlene Van Brocklin, a missionary in South America, says,

> Other new missionaries... derided our efforts to follow the meager orientation program our mission provided. "You mean you actually *read* those books on the orientation list?" But enthusiasm is appreciated by the people of our host country. A friend later laughed about our first attempts at speaking Spanish. She said, "The Mormon missionaries come with a rote memory schpiel they've learned in fair Spanish. They give it and leave. You two *butchered* the language when you came but what you said was from the heart."

I have known people who are brilliant at observing culture and formulating it, particularly at formulating it in ways that other Westerners will enjoy. But they are not always good at working within that culture. They understand it, but they have not really humbled themselves to it. They may play for rave reviews from their Western peers. They will certainly not play for rave reviews from the people they are attempting to explain. What Kenyan will admire me for grasping what is to him second nature? He will appreciate it if he sees me acting in an understanding and humble way. But he will not listen to me lecture on his culture. Nor is he likely ever to think of me as more fluent than he in his mother tongue. I am always his junior, at best his model student. Language learning reminds me of that, reminds me that humility is sheer realism.

A third blessing of learning a language is that you cannot learn it without mixing. Early stages can be learned in school. But eventually you have to spend many hours simply talking. Many forms of missionary work do not require that, but language learning does. The more you mix, the more likely you will make friends.

Finally, language gives a good gauge of how much you know the culture. It is tempting, as I have mentioned, to cut language learning short and launch into ministry. It is even more tempting to cut culture learning short. As soon as you can get by, you become a self-appointed expert on the local culture, lecturing helpless newer missionaries.

Polite people in the Third World may encourage you to think you know all about their culture. It is easy to fool yourself on this. I think you are less likely to fool yourself about language. If you can get by, you know it to be that and only that. You would not pose as an expert. Roughly speaking, most people know about as much of the culture as they do of the language—at least no more. So if you just "get by" in the local language, you probably can no more than "get by" in the local culture.

A Specimen of Failure

I began this chapter by referring to myself as a specimen of failure. My situation was exceptional in that my work did not require a second language. I was put in a two-week course, which gave me enough Kiswahili to say hello and inquire about someone's health. More than most people, I think, I was determined to go on, and I did devote a few minutes of each day to language study. But my base was not strong enough to enable me to converse freely. So when a Kenyan spoke English, I found it far easier to use that language.

The odd thing is that I spent the first year in Kenya doing informal research into the feasibility of a magazine. I could have done quite a lot of that research while studying language, for along with the language I would have picked up quite a lot of local culture. But I was in a hurry.

There I am sure I serve as a typical specimen. Learning a language is really quite simple: simply work. I know of no tricks to break down this barrier. You have to force yourself to devote time to it. You have to put yourself into situations where you must use it. The rewards are great, but they come slowly. Let this specimen be a lesson to others: be in no hurry to move on to other things. The time learning language is never wasted. It pays off in the freedom to make real friends.

6
When Values Clash

WE ARRIVE IN A NEW culture—all of us do—with ideas about the right way to do things. Some of these values we are aware of, but of others we are quite unconscious. Most of us, for instance, have never thought about why it is important to start meetings on time; we just know that it is.

Some of our values are biblical morality ("Thou shalt not steal"), and some are just the Western way of doing things. But when these Western values are violated, we often react as though someone had attacked the Bible. Another culture, with its different values, could help us re-examine our own. But often it just makes us angry.

Paul Buttrey writes:

I am aware of this [judgmental] attitude when I look at the tremendous amount of building going on. This represents population increase, affluence and growth in the urban areas. However, the standards of building are decidedly inferior to American standards. I see some of the shoddy work done and think, "How can they do that? Don't they have any pride in their workmanship?"

I find it easy to become quite agitated over these things which have no direct effect on my life. Sometimes I feel quite angry. I realize that if I let this type of critical spirit take over, it could create barriers between myself and Chinese friends here.

Here we strike a high and hard barrier. Cultures are different not just in superficials—the way we talk and eat and plan—but in essentials that touch on morality. Any alien culture will repel you at times, but even more it will morally offend you. To do shoddy work, you may say, is plain wrong. Perhaps it doesn't bother you in building standards, but what about in medical standards? I never knew a Westerner working in Kenyan hospitals who was not bothered deeply by this.

Appalled or Apathetic?
When you talk about such things to fellow missionaries, you will probably be rewarded with glum shakings of the head and stories more tragic than your own. If, on the other hand, you talk to national Christians, their reaction will probably not satisfy you. They may agree with you that shoddiness is shocking, but you will notice *they* do not seem shocked. They may have accepted shocking practices as normal and un-changeable, and not so important as they seem to you. They may even defend practices that seem to you indefensible. I once listened to a leading African Christian defend the practice of bribery.

We practice the same process of accommodation to our own culture. It is educational to talk to foreigners visiting the United States. They may be shocked by things we have long accepted, such as unfriendliness, pornography, children's disrespect for their parents, a lack of hospitality, a high divorce rate, a high rate of rape and murder, cancer or air pollution. To them these problems may be urgent. To you they may be "the price we pay for freedom," or the result of conditions too difficult or costly to change.

Missionaries of a century ago seemed to suffer little doubt about what to do when they found something they considered evil. What they did not approve of, they set out to change. Some of their changes seem now, at least, humorous, as in the case of the Scottish Presbyterians who taught the Kikuyu to give up their traditional dances and substituted lessons in Scottish folk dances. If nineteenth-century missionaries thought a people lazy, they set out to teach them industry. If they thought their scant clothing indecent, they clothed them. The idea was to make not only good Christians but good people of them. And given the missionaries' lack of cultural anthropology, who can say they were entirely wrong? Isn't it right to pass on virtues to others? I am told that some missionaries to Nigeria ran into trouble for the opposite fault: they discouraged Africans from adopting European ways, and Africans still remember them with resentment for "holding their people back." Perhaps there is no way to affect someone's culture and escape all blame.

The nineteenth-century course is not open to us, however, because the era of colonialism is over. We cannot impose our ideas. We will only alienate people if we try. Of course, missionaries still sway the cultures they work in, but more subtly, and often unintentionally. (Our electric appliances may have as much influence as our scruples on bribery.) Compared to our predecessors, we are impotent. We find things we do not like, but we cannot do a thing about them—except complain.

Roughly speaking, you can react to your impotence at one of two extremes. For one, you can sulk, very much like little boys who on realizing that no one cares to play their game withdraw and rehearse cutting remarks. It is easy to develop a dual life, making polite remarks when with your hosts, and comparing horror stories when you are with fellow Westerners. You will not draw close to your hosts this way.

The other extreme, commoner among younger, more liberal-minded missionaries, is to excuse everything. Where you see greed or embezzlement, you excuse it because of the tremendous poverty. Where you see promiscuity, you point out that Americans are also promiscuous. When bribery comes up, you mention Watergate and corporate bribery in the United States. When political violence is discussed, you refer to twenty million or more who died in World War 2.

Both reactions have this in common: they enhance your image of yourself. Those who sulk nurse feelings of superiority to the culture they are supposed to serve. Those who excuse evil nurse feelings of superiority to those who sulk. Neither is the reaction of someone genuinely engaged with a new culture. They are reactions at a distance, comments for a discussion. They do not help you know how to act when confronted directly with actions you believe to be wrong.

Fine China and Paper Plates

What should we do? We need first to clarify our understanding. There may be another side, which we do not see, to almost any moral outrage. What looks like shoddy work to us may be quite good enough for what it was intended. Paper plates are by one view shoddy, by another functional. No one confuses them with fine china, but that doesn't mean they are inferior.

We also need to understand our role. "We are guests of the country," some missionaries say, "and it is not our role to be involved in politics." They say this when someone questions their acquiescence to political brutality. To a point, they are right. No one has invited any missionary to come and overhaul the political or social system of his country. Anyone who tries may be counterproductive. His comments may not be welcomed any more than Americans welcomed criticisms coming from Iranian students who supported the Ayatollah Khomeini during the embassy hostage crisis.

But being a guest does not exempt you from being a human being. If as a guest in someone's home you discover a dead body, you are duty-bound to report it to the police, no matter how impolite and unwelcome that may seem to your host. We cannot be like the Pharisee in the story of the good Samaritan, by-passing trouble because it is not our role to get involved. If we live surrounded by injustice, we must stand for justice.

But just how are we to do so? We do not need to score debating points. The idea is to spread righteousness, and that is quite different from talking about it.

I would like to give three illustrations. I do so hesitantly, because I am unsure I understand them completely. All I know is that I understand them more than I did. I want to show not the "right" answers I arrived at, but the process I began toward developing understanding. The process continues, and my conclusions are tentative. Probably they always will be. I have deliberately chosen subjects that are not easy to treat neatly.

The first can be labeled "laziness." The term is a judgment, of course, and that is why I put it in quotes. It stands for people who, to the eye of a Westerner, do not work hard or productively. Anyone who has lived in the Third World can tell you stories of officials who think they earn their salaries by sitting in a chair; of sullen clerks in dusty offices reading the newspaper; of men who drink tea and watch the sun's progress while their wives chop weeds in the fields. Westerners adjust to this either by doing everything for themselves, or by slowing to a lazy, unproductive pace. They make little ironic jokes about doing things on "African time," which "stretches and compresses on an infinite scale, like bubble gum."

It is tempting to excuse all this, as (1) we surely have lazy bureaucrats in the West (the slowest moving object, we used to say, is a parcel moving from one bin to another in the Chicago post office); and, at any rate, (2) a sense of time is relative to a culture. Such excuses are fine, so long as we keep our feet planted firmly in the air. At a more practical level, low productivity works against what people want. In theory there is no "right speed," and a society which values leisure and time-consuming social relationships will naturally move more slowly. But in practice you find that all over the Third World the same people who move slowly crave "development," which is usually synonymous with wealth. They cannot get it without hard, efficient work. There may be no guarantee of wealth if they work hard. But there is a guarantee of poverty if they do not.

The system which encourages laziness and inefficiency often keeps the corrupt elite in power, too. The way to advance in your career is through favors from the right people; good work goes unrewarded. In many parts of the world the first thing you do when you enter an office is look for a friend or relation. This practice ensures that people from remote places or small and unfavored ethnic groups get nowhere, for they have no friends or relations in the office. If a government clerk is too lazy to process all applications, but only manages those of his friends, he effectively keeps certain people on top and certain others on the bottom.

Slowing Down

But a missionary coming to work in a Third World country doesn't see things analytically. He just discovers that things don't go so quickly as they did at home. This is partly because the system is different and he doesn't know how to work it, and partly because poverty keeps old and poorly maintained equipment working long after it ought to have been retired. But some of the difference, in the church as well as in the government, seems rooted in people's attitudes. They don't seem to care about working hard and efficiently to get everything done on time.

An older missionary may say, "Things just don't get done too fast here; take it easy." The advice is not necessarily bad, depending on how it is taken. If it means that there is no point getting hot under the collar when things don't get done on your schedule, it is good advice. If it means that as the new kid in town it does not become you to make snap judgments or complaints, it is good advice. But if it implies a patronizing attitude toward the people you work with, it is not good advice; it is disastrous, for it solves the problem by putting a barrier between you and the people you work with. You need not try to understand them anymore, just to coexist with them. There are no roots of respect in the unspoken thought that "these people just can't work like we do," and without respect no relationship can flourish.

I puzzled over what I saw. "These people are lazy" didn't seem accurate to me. If I drove to the airport in the early morning I would find the road, which also leads to the industrial area, jammed with thousands of workers. They walk a good five miles to their factory jobs. Was this laziness? The man who gardened for us every Monday worked tirelessly, usually refusing lunch, for about $3 a day. Others did the same. Was that laziness? I saw how hard the women worked in the countryside. Certainly they were not lazy.

Part of the "laziness" we see is our selective perception. Emi Gichinga, a Kenyan, wrote me,

> This concept about Africans has been perpetuated in many Western writings. It offends. Sometimes I feel African women work harder than Western women. Western women have gas or electric stoves, electric irons, carpets, etc. An African woman has to light a wood or charcoal fire, collect firewood and water, milk the cows, etc. When they sit down to rest, is this laziness? We would call Western women lazy for spending a whole week mountain climbing, sitting along the beach, watching wild animals.

Still, in many government and private offices, productivity is low. And since I was trying to start a magazine office, what I saw was more than an annoyance. It raised practical questions about how to run an office, how to apply the work ethic to a real-life situation.

Fair Pay
The staff of *Step* magazine, whom I hired and trained, developed into one of the finest working groups I have ever

encountered. However, I found they had some attitudes toward work that I did not understand. They were all young people who lacked experience and training, but they were enthusiastic and eager to learn. As such, they worked hard. But I soon sensed that we had a problem over salaries.

We had set salaries at levels quite reasonable compared to other locally funded Christian groups—and compared to my own. I thought they were fair, considering the lack of experience our staff had. If *Step* did well, we hoped to see salaries rise substantially. But that depended on them. Even if American donors gave enough to pay higher salaries, the danger was that *Step* would establish itself at too high a level and then die once the donor money stopped. It had happened many times with other literature projects.

But the issue of salaries kept coming up, and though the discussion was polite, bitterness lay just around the corner. It took me a lot of time to understand the way things looked to them. Gradually, through discussion, this picture emerged:

Any company, organization or government, they felt, owes its employees a good salary. If it doesn't pay good salaries, it must feel contempt for its workers. You may expect this from non-Christian companies, but a Christian organization should be different. Christians should recognize how difficult it is to live on a limited salary. Christians should treat their workers well.

But a piece of the picture was missing—a piece that usually need not be mentioned in America because it is taken for granted. Nowhere in the picture was any idea of where the money came from. Nowhere could be found the realization that the hard work of the employees resulted in increased profits, which could be used to pay the employees more. The employees' work seemed unconnected to their salary. This attitude is bound to spread in any large bureaucracy. You could find it in many U.S. government offices, I am sure. But I was surprised to find it at tiny *Step* magazine, where you could see the whole organization and all its income at a glance.

A Christian organization ought to pay its employees fairly. A few times this point was made, indignantly, by the very accountant who had just shown me that we had no money in the bank. The relationship between that and salary levels did not click with him. I would point out that if we raised salaries we might all be out of a job. He would listen politely and then begin to recount again how difficult it was, with rising prices, to make ends meet. We were talking in parallel lines. In the end all I could say was that if someone felt cheated I would not blame him for seeking a better-paying job. I was pretty sure no one would find such a job; the economy was tough on everyone. But looking toward the future, I wondered how Kenyans with that attitude could take over leadership of the magazine.

I began to make an educational campaign of it, using numerous examples to try to make the whole staff see that money does not come from nowhere. We would talk, for instance, about government clerks. Some do almost no work at all in Kenya, but the clerks still feel strongly that the government ought to pay them well. You could point out that because so many don't work the government has to hire far too many, that taxation to pay the clerks reduces the productivity of the economy, resulting in low growth and high inflation, which in turn reduces government revenues so that there is no money to pay the clerks more. But to the clerk that is all talk. *The government ought to pay its clerks fairly.* Where the money comes from, he has not the slightest idea or concern.

So we talked about that. I tried to show them that Kenya was only as rich as the total sum of its production of eggs, milk, nails, houses and so on. If this sum did not grow, but government clerks got a raise enabling them to buy more, then necessarily someone else would be able to buy less.

I tried ceaselessly to apply such thinking to *Step*. I worked as a kind of exorcist, trying to drive "Step" (as a separate entity) out of their minds. They had in their minds the concept of *Step* as an organization that employed them and thus owed them certain benefits. I tried to show them they owed benefits to themselves, for they were *Step,* and *Step* was what they made of it. In this I think I succeeded, and a hard-working, enthusiastic office resulted. Perhaps this educational campaign was the most significant work I did.

I am not sure why this link is missing, though I suspect it has to do with colonialism. In living memory, white people, Indians or "the government" owned everything of significance. An African owned nothing, not even his country. He didn't work hoping to see something grow, but only to get a salary. I suspect the attitudes which grew then live to this day. When government and business are corrupt and autocratic, these attitudes are perpetuated. They may be, in many situations, quite realistic. Often hard work is not rewarded.

These attitudes do not, however, add up to laziness. Laziness is a moral failure; this problem has more to do with a perception of reality. You cannot really do much about laziness, except preach a sermon against it. But you can fruitfully discuss these attitudes and work to counter them. When you do, barriers between you and those you work with come down.

The Rubbing Stone of Independence
My second illustration has to do with politics. It did not take me long to see that Kenyans regard independence from Britain as the greatest achievement of their history. They had thrown off their oppressors, as had all other African countries excepting South Africa.

To many Westerners this seems inaccurate and even hypocritical. Colonists did a great deal to develop the economies of most countries they ruled. Some of those countries have actually gone backward economically since they got their treasured independence. Many have also gone backward politically. Compared to the brutal and autocratic regimes of some African countries today, the colonial governments appear relatively liberal. Even in the most liberal African countries you would not be wise to publicly criticize the president today; but the independence movements were built on such criticism of the colonial powers.

Yet Africans never seemed to doubt that independence had been not only right but divine. It was a rubbing stone they could return to again and again: "We did it before, and we will do it now." They regarded South Africa, on the other hand, as the seat of deepest evil. That its press was more liberal and its economy wealthier than theirs made no difference.

Few Westerners would want to defend South Africa or colonialism; but black Africa, many feel, is in no position to criticize. It too has racism, oppression, political prisoners and so on.

Yet Africans do criticize, fiercely. I puzzled over this and discussed it with African friends. This time I was the one who got educated. Through their strong feelings I came to understand better the universal human longing for freedom. As an American who had always had it, I had taken it for granted. But a glance through history reminded me that people always want to be governed by their own people; they would rather be misgoverned by their own leaders than governed well by foreigners. Occupying armies rarely last. Local tyrants often do.

When Napoleon invaded Russia, the crucial question was not whether he would govern Russia better than the czars. The only question driving men to fight and die was "Is he Russian?" Similarly, Ethiopians responded to Emperor Haile Selassie's call to fight the invading Italians not because they believed Italy would suppress freedom of speech. They responded because they believed Italians were not Ethiopians. American Indians, for that matter, fought against our forefathers' invasion not because they believed the U.S. Constitution was a flawed document. They fought and died believing that Indian land belonged to the Indians, to do with as they chose.

We, however, have governed ourselves for so long that we have forgotten what the privilege means. Good government has become a question of multiparty democracy, of constitutions and human rights. We forget that no constitution can make an occupation acceptable; no freedoms can placate people who are ruled by another people. In my wilder moments I can imagine Japan taking over the United States and finding ways to make us more productive, raising our standard of living and perhaps our standard of family life too. But I know it would make no difference what good they did us. We would not be grateful. We would fight to be free of them, no matter what it cost us.

No doubt Africans are somewhat myopic about colonialism. The subject is too close and emotional for objectivity. In the light of history, the British and the French will get their due as less than legendary dragons. They were, after all, only the latest of the marauding bands of history, and among the least malevolent. But that does not alter the fact that they were intolerable to the people they ruled. And South Africans, while having as much right as anyone to live in their land, cannot rule over black Africans as anything but foreigners. By contemplating African values which I did not understand, I came to understand my own values—and found them to be the same. What had been a barrier between us became a piece of common ground.

I realized that Africans do indeed have something to be fiercely proud of in their independence struggles. For these struggles, most of which were far less bloody than the American Revolution, prove that they maintained a crucial sense of dignity as a people. The humbling power of Western might, wealth and technology can hardly be exaggerated; Third World people might easily have given up and consigned themselves to the rule of these "superior" people. They did not. They demanded self-rule, knowing instinctively that people have the right to decide how to live, even if they do it "all wrong" by someone else's standard. God himself does not take away this right of self-determination, even when it leads us to rebel against him.

A Hated Minority

A third example, and one I am not nearly so satisfied with, has to do with Asians. "Asians," in East African speech, are Indians or Pakistanis. Many have lived in East Africa for generations and know no other home. They run many of the most prosperous businesses. And many Kenyans hate them. If an irresponsible government came to power, they would certainly suffer. In the chaos of the August 1982 coup attempt, mobs streamed directly to their homes, robbed their businesses and raped their women as though by a prearranged signal.

The complaints against Asians are frighteningly similar to those the Germans made about Jews before World War 2: Asians do not mix, they enjoy cheating people, they control the economy without any sense of national loyalty, and they treat Africans like dirt. These complaints have a measure of truth, but that does not stop me from wincing when I hear African Christians talk about Asians as though they were nonhuman. I have a terrible aversion to ethnic stereotypes and prejudice, perhaps because of what I have seen it do to America.

I listened to a good deal of such prejudice in Kenya. I found it hard not to become angry toward it; it seemed to be racism in as ugly and pure a form as I had ever seen it. I am still not sure I was wrong in thinking so. But several thoughts have tempered my reaction.

First, I came to see that the angle of our experiences makes a difference. I am extremely sensitive to racism. An American ought to be. We decimated the native peoples of our continent. We live with a terrible legacy of hatred between black and white. We are witnesses to the deaths of six million Jews. But to Africans, these are somebody else's sins—not theirs. They see little extraordinary in tension between different ethnic groups. Tribes are prejudiced against other tribes, races against races. It has been so for a thousand years, and it has not destroyed the fabric of society.

Perhaps they view ethnic hostility the way most people view

a man shouting at his wife. Occasionally a domestic quarrel flares into violence, even murder, but that does not mean you should call in the army every time a husband and wife exchange words. My sensitivity to the possibility of violence is valid, I think, but so may be their sense of the likelihood that life will go on as it has.

I also realized that Kenyans did, indeed, have a problem. Their government is still fragile. It must be seen to be fair, and not the tool of a small, self-perpetuating, indisputably foreign group like the Asians. Otherwise the consensus that supports it will disintegrate.

Yet large sectors of the economy are increasingly controlled by Asian families. They are clever business people, they have money and expertise, and they expect to hand over leadership to their sons. No African can expect to reach the top in an Asian business. Kenya is a small country, its urban economy extremely limited. If ninety-nine per cent of its people are denied access to half the urban economy, how could that seem fair? For Kenya to remain stable, the economy has to become better integrated.

When I began to grasp the complexity of these issues, and something of how they appeared to most black Kenyans, I was able to discuss them better. I am particularly grateful to my colleagues at *Step* magazine who talked with me at length. I discovered, as I did so often with other issues, that they shared many of my concerns. But they wanted first to make me understand that a problem existed. One result of our conversations was an issue of *Step* which dealt with the Asian problem in sensitive and Christian terms.

Spouting Off

I have offered these examples to suggest a process. We cannot ignore or excuse immorality and injustice, saying that we are only guests. But we need to oppose them with care—that is to say, effectively.

An American church of which I was a member once asked a

Nigerian student at a nearby college to speak to us. He spoke with great emotion against the promiscuous habits of young American Christians. He meant that he had seen them holding hands and even kissing in public. This is strictly taboo among most African Christians. After his talk, no one even bothered to discuss his views with him. The subject was too complex and our assumptions too different to go into.

No doubt that Nigerian felt he had done "his Christian duty," speaking prophetically to Americans. He relieved his own tension and frustration by spouting off. But he accomplished nothing. It is usually better to retain such tension while searching for a deeper understanding and a more creative way to promote change.

The first step of this process is to keep quiet and listen. You may express your views—no one objects to that—but you can express them as a question instead of as a harangue. Keep asking, keep listening, and reserve your conclusions. Keep quiet even with your fellow Westerners. It feels good to spout off among people who agree with you, but it works to harden your attitudes. You are only gossiping, anyway, unless you intend to band together to change those things you consider wrong.

Second, try to empathize. When you encounter something ugly, make the gracious assumption that you have not understood it. We desperately need the gift of imagination: to be able to mentally explore another person's position and try to understand how he sees it. When you see empathetically that there are many ways to understand someone's actions, many different sets of clothing to try on it, your mind gets too busy to condemn. Eventually you may understand better.

The third step is to understand your role. As a guest you are not exempt from responsibility, but your role is different. The values you propose become part of a larger struggle between two cultures. You cannot encourage local leadership while taking it from them. You cannot encourage them to think through difficulties while publicly pushing your solutions. You undercut them if you do.

We like to give answers. Perhaps our competitive school system encourages this. The teacher asks a question, and you wave your hand wildly hoping to be called. If someone else is chosen and answers correctly, you feel disappointed. If, though, he falters, your hopes rise again, and you shoot your hand skyward.

I have often seen this in Bible studies. Anyone who knows something about a passage feels he must say it. The leader flounders alone trying to assimilate diverse comments into some helpful direction. But other participants, particularly intelligent and knowledgeable ones, hardly ever ask themselves, "Is what I want to say helpful at this moment?" They only think about getting credit for a smart answer.

They disregard what the Bible says about words: that they can be dangerous, particularly if said in haste. The book of Proverbs teaches that a statement which is perfectly true and not directly harmful to anyone still ought not, sometimes, to be said. There is a right word for a particular moment, and other words may clutter up the air so that the right word is not heard.

So it is with us in the role of missionary. Each of us has particular things to say. We are not to say everything or do everything. God will provide others to say and do what must be said and done. We ought to pray, and think, and discuss with others what our place is.

The fourth and perhaps most important step is to find local Christians we can work with for change. If something is truly wrong, God will not keep it a secret between you and him. He has probably put it on the conscience of others, too. They may be lonely people who need encouragement and support in opposing their own people. They may be baffled as to how to proceed. You can work as partners, supporting each other. (They must not be mere assistants recruited to help you in your reforming crusade.) With them you can refine a message and approach so it speaks accurately and clearly. And through them the message is far more likely to be heard. Teamwork is slower than spouting off. But it has a long-lasting effect.

Partnership for Change

Such partnership, I am sorry to say, is not universal. The differences in our values do not always drive people together to share understanding. A missionary may say he loves the people he works with, and yet be bitterly critical—with a shrug—of their values. Such missionaries rarely effect change. They merely build walls.

But there are more hopeful cases. Missionaries do become partners for change in many small ways—and a few large ones. They affect thinking about honesty, about interracial fairness, about hard work, about compassion. Occasionally they have opportunity to stand, with national Christians, against something which would destroy a nation's hopes.

I think of the 1969 Oathing Crisis in Kenya, a severe moment of testing. A revered political leader, Tom Mboya, had been murdered. Many believed that leaders in the Kenyatta government were responsible. The nation was tense, and Kikuyu leaders, with government approval, began resurrecting the Mau Mau oath. This time it was not against whites but against the other tribes of Kenya. They would force Christian Kikuyu to take it; they killed some who refused, and beat and injured many. A handful of Christian leaders stood virtually alone against this. In particular one church in Nairobi, which had an integrated leadership, was instrumental in breaking the oath's back. They could not have done so without partnership. Their white pastor could not have understood the implications of the oathing unless Kikuyu men and women had explained it to him, for the subject was absolutely secret. Most probably, no individual member of the congregation could have safely made public statements against the oathing. The pastor did, and got away with it. They campaigned openly for every church in Kenya to take a different oath—one of allegiance to Jesus. It was a truly heroic moment of courage under persecution. The oathing stopped.

But such crises come suddenly; there is no time to build a dialog if one has not already begun. Now is the time to begin the process of understanding those values we cannot accept. Now is the time to build relationships that enable us to effectively work as partners for change.

7
Colonialism: A Persistent Complaint

AYOUNG WOMAN ONCE wrote me a letter confessing that she had harbored bitterness toward me for years. Fortunately she described the offending incident in some detail, because even with that jog to my memory I could only hazily remember her. I had been staying with some family friends, and she had been introduced to me. "Oh," she wisecracked, "you're the famous writer Tim Stafford." According to her, I drew back as though she were a snake, and I hardly acknowleged her existence for the short time she was there until she left. I had been a plague on her mind ever since.

Although I could barely remember the event, I could guess what my reaction had been. I am fundamentally shy, and I do not feel terribly secure about my gifts as a writer. Her comment must have embarrassed me. Not knowing how to respond, I had withdrawn from her. From my perspective, I had not deliberately slighted her. I had just been self-conscious. The encounter had not been a significant one, and I had immediately forgotten it. From my view she had blown it up out of proportion, imagining motives that had not crossed my mind.

The Sin of Not Noticing
The young woman's perspective was quite different. She hoped to become a writer. Anyone who has that hope knows the loneliness and uncertainty which accompany it. Perhaps she had problems with her self-acceptance anyway. I represented success to her, and she had tried to acknowledge that in her own way, with something short of social skill. If I was self-conscious, she was more. From her perspective my withdrawal conveyed lack of respect. I had communicated, "I am not interested in you. You do not matter." Representing (to her) the powers she longed to impress as an equal, I had reinforced her worst fears about herself. Was I really, under the best interpretation, innocent? I had failed to take an interest in, and understand sympathetically, another human being who needed my encouragement.

An objective observer examining my behavior might ask further questions. Was my behavior typical? Did I merely lapse, or do I act that way consistently? He might want to go even further. Was my action typical of members of my class, that is, of writers? Were we in fact a tight-knit, proud group that took little note of those struggling to join us?

But I prefer to see it from my point of view, which seems perfectly reasonable to me. I don't like being classed as a symbol of someone's ambitions and fears. I would rather be taken for what I am, no more and no less. If others make their living the same way I do, does that make me responsible for their actions? Let me be judged on my own merits, please.

But in fact I am a member of many classes of people. I am a writer, so would-be writers may approach me with some envy or admiration. I am a Christian, so non-Christians will approach me with stereotyped expectations. I am a man, so women will size me up as a member of my sex. I am a Westerner, so people in the Third World will look at me as representative of Western society. They will see me through the glasses of history—through slavery, colonialism, paternalism and exploitation. I don't like being seen this way, any better than I liked being a scourge on a would-be writer's mind. But I do not see any way we can avoid being classed, whether fairly or not. History forms a barrier to any missionary wanting to make friends in a culture that knows his own culture all too well. Whether we agree with their point of view or not, we do well to understand it.

I hasten to say that I am not trying to make a strict parallel between my slight of the young woman and colonialism. The complaint about colonialism is, to say the least, more grave. It involves many incidents on the level of my slight—hurt feelings, offended dignity. But it also includes the actual sale of human beings, large-scale murder, political repression and economic exploitation of whole peoples.

My incident with the would-be writer does, however, tell something about the difference in two points of view. To me, the incident was nothing. It was nothing because she meant nothing to me. I didn't know her. But to her the incident was everything. She knew me, and I represented something important to her.

So it will be between the West and the Third World. A rare Westerner has thought about it in personal terms. If he has learned about colonialism in a classroom, he thinks an African (or South American, or Vietnamese) should congratulate him for being so aware of the faults of his grandfathers. He cannot see why an African should be suspicious of *him*. Africa is nothing to him; he has no ambitions there.

But to anyone in the Third World, Western culture forms a dominant issue in national, family and even personal life. An educated person must try, while maintaining his traditional ties, to succeed in an increasingly Westernized society.

The exercise is highly strenuous. What seems insignificant to me may be highly emotional to him. Offense can be taken where none is intended.

When I think of the young woman, I feel grateful she was willing to write and tell me what she felt. It took boldness. She was trying to shake her own bugaboo, but she helped me in the process. Probably I have offended others in the same way, but my offense lies hidden from me. Had she not told me, I would never have thought of it. We accrue a kind of compound interest on our hidden sins. We do the same thing again and again, without knowing it. Westerners in the Third World, in similar fashion, repeat mistakes because they are ignorant of the history that went before.

An Old, Old Story

It may be helpful, then, to sketch the story of European colonialism and try to suggest how it looks to someone from a former colony. Whether their view is completely historically accurate is not my point. We need to know how they see their past, for we fit into their picture.

It is an old, old story. To the strong go the spoils. One marauding band or another has always been tramping onto someone's land. Europeans made only the latest and most successful example.

Beginning with the Spanish and Portuguese explorers, European powers established commercial interests all around the world, fighting each other and whomever they met for territory and trade. The whole world was a field for them to prove themselves on, and only a few nations like Japan were strong enough to keep them outside the door.

This surge of power from Europe to the rest of the world gradually died. In the Americas, the children of the colonizers themselves declared independence—and fought for it. Most of Africa and Asia had to wait until after World War 2 to claim independence. A change of weather came then, and in a few short years the European powers gave up virtually all the lands they had controlled for centuries.

Each former colony has its distinct history, determined not just by local conditions but by the strategy of its colonizing power. Some European powers raped the land, while others built schools. Some intermarried with local people; others did not. Some settled on the land as farmers; others merely administered large territories. The French made their colonies eerily French; the British made theirs oddly British. North and South America share a colonial history completely different from that of Africa and Asia, for in the Americas the children of the colonizers were not driven out but themselves fought for independence.

After independence, in what is sometimes called the neocolonial era, came more uniformity. No longer were the former colonies shaped by the narrow national interests of their masters. Now any commercial power was free to operate. French companies entered British colonies and vice versa. More significantly, as companies competed in an international market they began to operate more and more similarly, becoming less national. Eventually many stopped being subject to any country at all. They became "multinational."

In this neocolonial situation, each former colony is politically independent. In theory they are no longer subject to anyone. But culturally and economically they remain under the sway of the vast wealth and knowledge of the West. Whether they like it or not, their chief preoccupation must be to incorporate and sift this Western influence while maintaining and redefining their national traditions. A few Marxist countries have sealed their borders, but even this is a response to Western influence—a totally negative one. And Marxism, too, is an influence the West must claim credit for.

For people who still remember when independence came, colonialism and neocolonialism are all mixed up. These people do not separate the sins of our grandfathers, as colonists, from the sins of Exxon today. We are one people to them— the ruling people. Their one great event of history was political independence from us. They go on struggling for cultural and economic independence. The political struggle we give all our attention to—Washington vs. Moscow—they see mainly in the context of their own nationalistic goals. Many see both great powers as having the same aim—domination of the small and weak, whether militarily, economically or culturally.

In many parts of the world, and particularly among the young and educated, a Marxist-Leninist interpretation of colonialism has had tremendous influence. Lenin interpreted colonialism as a way for industrial nations to remove the class struggle outside their national borders. Instead of exploiting a worker class among their own people, they would exploit workers in defenseless countries far away. The Third World, according to this interpretation, has become the working class for the industrialized world. These "classes" will naturally struggle against each other, and this "class struggle" will take the form of wars of national liberation.

Whether this theory is right or wrong, it attracts many people in the Third World. It asserts that they are not underdeveloped because they are backward—an implication they cannot miss in the thinking of many Westerners. They are underdeveloped because the West exploits them. It is someone else's fault, not theirs. Furthermore, since Marxism posits an inevitable triumph of the workers, their future is hopeful. Someday they will gain power. This sounds better than the prediction of most Western economics, which assumes they will lag behind for a long time.

Most of the colonies have had, since Lenin's writing, their wars of national liberation. They are proud of their independence. What do they expect of their government? They expect them to keep the foreign powers at bay, economically and culturally as well as politically. For the foreign powers, they feel, are naturally their exploiters.

You will observe this thinking any time a large-scale factory is envisioned, such as a paper mill. An American is likely to start by asking whether private enterprise or government would manage it more efficiently. But people in the Third World will not usually put the question that way. They will see their government as the only protector against exploitative foreign forces. The power and efficiency of multinationals they see as sinister. They will rarely think of a popular government, no matter how inefficient or corrupt, as potentially so malignant as these. Colonialism taught them that foreign forces will try to exploit and dominate them. Marxism (and nationalism) suggest that the control of the state is the preferred defense. The only question is whether the government is strong enough to put up a defense. In the case of the paper mill, can the government find enough money and expertise to start it, or will they be "forced" to rely on the multinationals?

The Opiate of the People

You may be impatiently wondering what this has to do with missionaries. Here is the answer: Marxism has tied Christianity to the cause of these foreign forces. Religion is the opiate of the people, Marxists say, supported by the rich to sedate the poor. Missionaries, then, are agents of capitalism. By introducing Christianity, they destroyed the local social structure. By founding schools they trained clerks for their businesses. By teaching submission to government, they pacified resistance to colonialism. (Marxism, of course, teaches a far more radical submission to government, but to the "workers'" government.)

This theoretical view of missionaries is probably little known outside universities. But it has slipped into common belief in many Third World countries, perhaps because so often missionaries were observably close to the commercial, colonial interests when they came. The trader and the missionary were not far from each other's path. In China, for instance, Christianity came along with opium traders. A war was fought by the British forcing the Chinese to accept these traders. Whenever missionaries got into danger, that same colonial army came, if it could, to rescue them. Naturally, many Chinese thought of missionaries as part of "them" rather than "us."

Today, many missions seem to continue in the neocolonial mold. In the classic neocolonial situation, a nation is given independence on paper but is still controlled by foreign companies and governments because of their vast wealth and power. They corrupt local officials to let them do what they want.

Some missions parallel that. On paper, the national church is independent. But everybody knows that the mission still controls things. Missionaries have money and education, the resources to start and maintain programs. Naturally, what they want to do they can do: who would stop them? It is all for a good cause. But the result is a national church which feels dominated by a foreign church.

There is a cast of characters to flesh this out. First come the Aggressive Americans. (They can come from any country, really.) They are friendly, well trained and respectful toward national leaders. But they have plans. They step off the airplane with plans. Usually these are similar to programs they have seen work at home. They assume any country could use them. These plans invariably require organization, further planning, committees, money and technology. Brochures must be printed. Videocassettes would be extremely useful. The schedule must be planned to the minute. These missionaries are eager to incorporate local thinking; list your suggestions and they will discuss how they can be worked in.

Programs to Match the Spirit

Nothing is really wrong with this, except that it is very, very Western. Often the planning, money and know-how make results. But often it is a result that cannot be sustained without the missionary because the program does not match the spirit of the local people. To a degree such missionary enthusiasm parallels that of the colonial trader or government officer, promising wonderful benefits, offering bright-colored beads, but betraying limited interest in local thinking. They will discuss local ideas but, be assured, they will make the final decisions.

Such missionaries do not necessarily meet resistance. Third World people may be too polite for that. Mary Jeanne Buttrey writes,

The emphasis in America so often seems to be to discover *the* gimmick that will ensure instant success. Hence the profusion of "how-to" books, especially in Christian bookstores. More and more I question that approach at home, but it obviously appears even more absurd on the mission field. One of our coworkers related an incident in the church she was attending while in language school. A group came from the States for a two- or three-week evangelism project, and the church essentially hosted them. Their goal was to train the church members in a particular method of evangelism. They of course had to depend on translators.

This church also happens to be an active one itself. Our friend observed what was going on and finally cautiously sounded out one of the older influential ladies in the church, wondering if this particular evangelism method was culturally appropriate. The lady's reply was basically, "We know, dear, we know." Here was a church which graciously helped this group because they had the resources to do so, but not because they needed or wanted the help the group came to give. I'm afraid people sitting at home get a great idea about going to some exotic place to turn it upside down for the Lord. They just don't realize that their pet solution may have nothing whatsoever to offer the people they want so much to help.

In such a polite environment, they will rarely be told so. And local people will always rise to work with them. Often these local people have something to gain: a higher salary, a chance for education, an opportunity to travel. I don't mean they are insincere. They are just malleable and can fit in with Western ways. Such nationals are cooperative and friendly, and often capable; but they are seldom really leaders.

In my experience, the people we most need to know are not so easily met. They are not malleable, but neither are they constantly spouting off their opinions. They have their own interests and their own programs. They keep them at a distance from foreigners. They feel no great need to talk to us, whether to elicit our support or to protest our shortsightedness. They behave politely until things reach such a state that they simply have to speak.

I arrived in Nairobi not long after an American Christian group had organized an evangelistic outreach for the whole city. The organization is large and well organized, and they had spent a lot of money to coordinate all types of media for a huge evangelistic thrust. They had managed to win initial cooperation from nearly all the Nairobi churches. Unfortunately, they had not listened carefully enough to some of the national leaders. Tension had reached a point where an old and much respected Kenyan leader, who had worked closely with them, denounced their tactics from the pulpit of his church. Repeatedly I heard from Kenyans, "We tried to talk to them, but they did not listen. They always went ahead with their plans."

Yet the leaders of the organization were convinced that the thrust had been a model of evangelical cooperation. They really had no idea anything had gone wrong. I can understand why. Nobody pounded the table. Nobody except one old pastor spoke "clearly" against them. Their support from key leaders just faded away. Because they had money and workers, they could do without it; they just pushed on, thinking perhaps that the Kenyan brothers were not very good at following up on their commitments. As a result they are a marked organization. They are seen, fairly or unfairly, as a Christian version of neocolonialism, trying to impose a foreign order through vast wealth and technical competence.

This view undoubtedly covers other mission groups as well, and other missionaries.

An Overpainted Picture

I have painted a bleak picture—overpainted it, I am sure. Nowhere I have been or heard about is the atmosphere charged with suspicion. If you were working at a university or in a country with a new, radical government, you might be called on to defend yourself. But mostly these issues lie quiet. That is part of the danger, though. They lie quiet, and you may easily overlook them.

My first year in Nairobi I was elated at how graciously we were received. Kenyans were warm, friendly and encouraging. Not until our fourth year did we see the degree of suspicion that lay underneath. I listened to groups of Christians talk heatedly about the government "selling" the country to foreigners. Some of the finest Christians I know were wishing the country had kicked out all missionaries years before. They weren't directing their comments at me. But it was painful to hear. You cannot divorce yourself from your own people, no matter how much you disapprove of the way they act. I was more surprised than pained, though. I had known such feelings existed. But I hadn't known they were felt so strongly by these people who had welcomed us from the beginning.

You cannot undo history. We are continually victims of it. The sins of the fathers are still visited on the children up to the third and fourth generation. Perhaps the greatest frustration in being a missionary rests here: you will never completely fit in.

Most of the world would not find this strange, but we Westerners are used to being the lucky ones of history. We cry, "It's not fair!" as though we had made a discovery. People who live in chronic, grinding poverty, or whose government may never approach any ideal of justice, will not pity us much.

History is part of the raw material we work with. Every field has its rocks. So when we talk about solutions, we are not discussing a magic wand to make problems disappear. If history has given us a broken leg, we want crutches to make it easier to move around and paths we can negotiate. In those terms, we can do a good deal about history.

First of all, we can read. Quite a lot of literature about nearly every part of the world can be found. You can learn an area's history. If the culture has produced literature, you can become familiar with its writers. You can gather anthropological information and learn the local geography. Knowing these things helps, if only to prove convincingly your interest in the people and place you are in. The books are often written by Westerners or by nationals heavily influenced by Westerners, and they may not help you see the landscape the way local people do or feel about history as local people do. But you can at least learn bare facts, which form a base that helps in gathering further information.

Second, you can make a point of heaping respect on respect toward the people and land you are in. You may feel it is "honest" to make critical observations. But recall that the West has been making critical observations about "primitive" and "unsanitary" people for centuries. Your hosts are aware of them even if you are not. In giving respect, you are making up for history in a tiny way. It may open some doors for you. Criticism is sure to close doors.

Third, you should seek people who will be frank with you. They will rarely be people you work with. Because of your educational qualifications, you will outrank most of your colleagues, and most people are hesitant to level with their superiors. You should surely be skeptical of people who praise the West too much, who love America or Europe and criticize their own people. Look for people, usually your peers educationally or socially, who will tell you things you do not want to hear. Look for people who strike you as a little bit hard to know, a little bit difficult to work with. In some cultures such people may be plentiful, but in many parts of the world they stay on the periphery of mission circles.

Blow on It!

An elderly Kenyan leader, John Mpaayei, once gave me advice I found extremely helpful. When I asked him for counsel at the beginning of my time in Kenya, he spoke with great warmth of the wonderful work missionaries had done. I think a slight twinkle came into his eyes. "The problem we have had," he said, "is that some of the missionaries have been such powerful, skillful personalities they have tended to overwhelm our people. We have been intimidated by your capabilities." Here he paused and looked straight at me. "If you see the smallest spark of initiative . . . blow on it." He paused and repeated himself. "Any spark . . . Blow on it! Blow on it."

In our work we are often charged with training a national replacement for ourselves. We feel a natural tendency to protect the work we have been given. A young replacement usually lacks our experience and background, and he or she is certain to do things differently from our way. Seeing this, a missionary may wait too long to give authority and so discourage those with the greatest potential and initiative. These give up and quit. A malleable remnant who lack the strength of character to lead stay on. This is one reason—there are many others, and the subject is complex—why nationalization of mission work has sometimes failed.

This is not the place to examine that entire issue. I merely contend that some such failures began with relationships that never got beyond stereotypes and suspicions. They never got beyond history, and they contributed more to a history that was hardly good to begin with. To erase that history, we need to take risks early in trusting people. It is better to fail that way than in its opposite, by trusting too little or too late.

Colonialism is really the sin of not noticing people. The earliest colonists made the mistake of thinking that, since the people they met had no guns or roads or machines, they could have no ideas either. I really suspect they hardly noticed the people they were stepping on. We may repeat the same mistake, thinking that people without know-how or efficiency to match ours are therefore children who must be taught. We will wound them if we think like that, just as I wounded my would-be writer without intending to, simply by not noticing she was there, by not caring about the particular sensitivities of her point of view. We will build the barrier of history higher and stronger if we act that way.

But the barrier of history can come down, at least on an individual basis. Someone who does listen, who tries his best to understand, will not go unnoticed. He will stand out from the pattern of history.

I think of Dave Ivaska, who trained Bible study leaders in East African universities. He would normally take the leaders through a model study. One study he often did asked for a definition of sin. When he asked the group what they thought of as "sin," they would invariably begin with the sins of South Africa, of Harlem, of Vietnam.

University students being what they are, they tested him. They would see if he would accept sin as an American phenomenon. When he quietly accepted those descriptions of sin, they went on to discuss sin's relevance to their own country and their own lives. But they had to make their point first.

It was a small thing he did, but history is an accumulation of small things. In his work, at any rate, history turned a corner. He was accepted and appreciated as few Americans have been in African universities.

Nonuniversity people will seldom be so obviously critical. But they too watch to see how we react, and they make judgments. Will we continue as part of the pattern of history? Or in us will they see history turn in a new direction?

8
Who's in a
Hurry?

I TALKED RECENTLY to a new missionary about to join a team in Lisbon, Portugal. The team had been there four years, trying to plant a church among the high-rise apartment buildings. The work was not progressing very quickly. The six missionary families had only a handful of converts to show. "They're having a hard time knowing what to put in their prayer letters," the missionary said. Their supporters, she felt, expected more.

Occasionally a missionary finds himself holding a tiger by the tail. Everything he tries takes off with brilliant success. But more often he finds himself pushed from slow gear into slower and then slowest. This makes quite a shock to your system when you had imagined doing all the things you had read about in missionary biographies.

Difficulties

One reason for the slow speed is that most missionaries do pioneer work, and such work is usually slow and faltering. It has always been so. Pick any missionary biography you like, and pay attention to the years of work that are described in a single paragraph: thousands of miles covered on foot or on a mule, a house built from local stone, a language learned from scratch. These are slow and boring tasks under the best of circumstances. Pioneers walk, their children drive, and their grandchildren fly.

Even those of us who fly make pioneers. We may pioneer a new accounting system. It may be tried and true in the United States, but take it to a mission field and what looks like a simple job can become next to impossible. Computer paper may be unobtainable for months at a time. Assistants you planned to train to run the system may suddenly seem impossibly thickheaded. Mold may grow on the disks. Voltage fluctuations may short the circuits. You can write one prayer letter mixing humor and a slightly desperate tone, but what do you say in your third and fourth prayer letters?

Let us be frank and say that, no matter how much our supporters at home trust us, we want to please them. As more and more missionaries raise their finances on a personal basis, they may feel this pressure intensify. You expect a mission board to understand the difficulties you face. But individual supporters who have never lived overseas lack the resources to understand. They may sympathize, but they will naturally think of a missionary's work in terms of what they would expect at home.

The pressure of these expectations—our own as well as our supporters'—creates underlying anxiety. We made sacrifices to become missionaries, and we certainly expected to accomplish something in doing so. It comes as a frightening surprise to realize we might not. We look around for someone to blame. This pressure may form a barrier between us and the people we have come to help. We are in a hurry; they are not.

From Frustration to Fury

I remember quite well the first time I went to pick up a package at the Nairobi post office. I came back bursting with the unbelievable story of how I had stood in five different lines and had my postal slip stamped and checked and figured on by eight different individuals, all to collect a small gift a friend had sent. The process took more than an hour. In the course of that hour I had gone from frustration to fury to resignation—and back to fury again. Just about any missionary working in the Third World could tell similar stories.

But you adjust. Eventually we learned to take a book or magazine with us. We learned to enjoy watching newcomers —Americans, Germans, Japanese—gesture and get red in the face, sometimes shouting as they encountered the bureaucracy for the first time.

I am not sure there is any logic behind this system, but I believe it meant to counteract widespread bribery. People might illegally import items through the mail if they had to deal with only one clerk. Convincing eight to cheat together is more difficult and expensive. I would not press the search for logic behind slowness, however. A good part seems to be simply cultural bias. We Westerners demand that things move quickly. Other people do not seem to notice.

The pioneer work missionaries do would be slow enough. But a less time-oriented culture slows us down much further and increases our frustration and anxiety. We can become greatly at odds with our hosts.

Neither our bias nor theirs is necessarily wrong, just different. Our Western bias in favor of speed has helped make our countries wealthy. If Third World people want to become wealthy like us, they may have to adopt our biases. But they have not yet done that, in most cases, and therefore our differences make a barrier between us.

We have a bias for time over event. That is, we expend considerable energy to schedule things. We discipline ourselves to force the haphazard events of the day to fit an invarying time sequence. I get to the office at 8:00 even if I knock my coffee cup on the floor just before leaving, and even if my father arrives at my door for a visit at 7:30. I leave the coffee spilled if necessary, and I can put my father off until another day. Time has become more important to me than events or people.

But for many people, events are the prime reality. Time is merely the elastic string connecting them. If someone's father appears at his door, he recognizes it as an event which must be lived fully before the next event can occur.

We have a bias for the result over the procedure. That is, unless immoral means are involved, the ends justify the means. But to many people the route you take to your destination matters just as much as the destination itself. I learned this while bargaining for fruit in Kenya. I enjoyed haggling over prices. It made a pleasant and sociable way to conduct business. The seller would name a ridiculous price, and through laughter and discussion we would reach a realistic compromise.

But sometimes I was in a hurry. I knew the approximate price our discussion would lead to, and I would try to take a short cut there. "You know this is a fair price. I don't have time to discuss it with you. Why don't you accept it now?" It never worked. Unless I had earned the lower price through a full discussion, I could not get it. I suspect the seller realized at some subliminal level that, if no discussion were necessary, he would not have a job. Buying and selling would become a cold and impersonal business, with price the only variable. That's how selling is in America.

I saw the value placed on proper procedure more clearly in the extensive negotiations a young man went through to "buy" a wife. Large delegations from his home village had to visit the girl's home several times for lengthy meetings, and the negotiations could drag on over months. Most of the time the result was predictable. Sooner or later the girl's father would give in with permission to marry. The amount of money he demanded would normally end up within the means of the young man. What you could not predict was how long he would take to reach this point. Negotiation took on a life of its own. Elaborate speeches had to be made, gifts produced, demands countered. In Africa, you do not court a girl but her father.

Americans would never have the patience for all that procedure. But in the process of negotiation, subtler things occurred. The two families got to know each other. The patience and maturity of the would-be groom and his family were tested. The girl was praised to the sky by all parties. The process had value of its own, value that would enhance the meaning of the end result, a marriage.

We have, finally, a bias for work over relationships. We would rarely keep someone in a job that he was not doing well just because we were afraid of hurting him. But in many parts of the world that is not so. You will find church leaders, for instance, who are quite incapable of doing their work. Why are they still in office? Because the damage done in removing them would seem much greater than the damage they do by staying.

In a hundred ways relationships get in the way of work. Relatives or friends will be given jobs whether they can do them or not. A family member calls to talk? Business stops until he is cared for. To our hosts this is a basic politeness, but many Westerners find it maddening. And it certainly slows us down in the work we plan to do. We are the people with plans, people who know how to get things done. And yet, often, we do not get done what we wanted to. This makes us edgy and unpleasant to be with.

The Bias for Speed

What can we do about this barrier? We are not going to shed our bias for speed. It is too deep a part of us. And our bias can actually be helpful to our hosts, for it does see things accomplished. We want to keep our bias, but keep it in a way that stops scraping against the opposite bias of our hosts.

That means, first of all, retaining a balanced view. Life does go on in the Third World. Fields do get plowed. People do eat. Roads are built; goods are produced. Churches grow. These things may not happen just the way we would wish, but they do happen. Third World people find ways to cope with interruptions—ways we can learn from.

We need, second, to understand why our hosts' priorities are different from ours, so that even while keeping our own we see the good in theirs. Anne Morrow Lindbergh's comment regarding her expectations in Mexico is helpful. "I don't know how I will react or how the people will react to me, but I do go expecting to like the people and to like their way of doing things."

If you look at the cultural biases I mentioned—time over event, result over procedure, work over relationships—you see they are all, in practice, against people. We want to be on time for the big meeting, so we ignore the neighbor who comes to visit at an inconvenient time. We want to get to the point, so we squash the wheezy old man who is droning on into eternity. We have a lot of work to do, so we demand that our secretary stop using the phone to call her husband. We have good reasons for all these decisions, but they are against people. Our hosts perceive us, then, as not caring for people.

We could use the flavor of their view. For what are our goals if not for people? How can a church be built if not through people? How can development occur if not through the ingenuity and interest of people? How can evangelism have lasting results if not through relationships? In our home countries people know us, they understand the way we think, and they trust us. But in a foreign context, no one knows us, no one trusts us, and most importantly no one understands us. We can only come to be known, trusted and understood as we build relationships. Our anxiousness to accomplish something may actually interfere with our productivity by keeping us from building those relationships.

It is a tricky business, keeping goals straight, moving ahead with work, while being sensitive not to tread on people or ignore opportunities to relate to them.

Marlene Van Brocklin suggests a down-to-earth example from her experiences in Bolivia.

It can be so annoying that just the basics of living take up *so* much time. I remember my chagrin when I learned that the only way to receive or post mail was to take a bumpy twenty-minute bus ride to the downtown La Paz post office. But I learned to enjoy those trips. It was a great place to run into people I knew. It's good to see all the errands you have to do as more opportunities to meet people and learn more about the culture. In our LAMP language learning course the Brewsters suggested that instead of buying the whole grocery list at one stop, we spread it out over three or four just for the extra contact with people.

Van Brocklin realized that what she initially saw as taking time from her ministry was really crucial to it.

I was helped tremendously at one time of discouragement by a visit from Robert Reekie of the David C. Cook Foundation, which specializes in Christian literature. He came to Nairobi when I was doubting whether *Step* magazine would make it financially. Problems with advertising revenue, printing costs and sales figures filled my conversation as I poured out my fears to him. He listened carefully but made few suggestions.

Reekie did, however, encourage me about the work. He seemed to figure that, whether or not *Step* magazine survived, the training I did with staff and writers would prove valuable. That training, he seemed to think, was more important than the magazine itself.

At first his attitude shocked me. He didn't seem to care about the really important thing, the magazine. But as he talked I began to re-evaluate my work. What would endure? Even a successful magazine rarely lasts thirty years. In Kenya the chances of such longevity were even smaller. But if *Step* left some writers, editors and artists trained and inspired to go on, that would have certain lasting value. *Step* mattered, but as much because of the people involved as because of the magazine itself. Really, the two were inseparable. In no way could *Step* thrive and endure without people of Christian character who knew how to run it and adapt it to ever-changing circumstances.

We set our goals in the first place because we think they are ultimately good for people. But along the way the goals can begin to run right over people. Then we need to reset our compass.

Sometimes the change is subtle. I needed to keep on publishing *Step,* but I needed to see developing people as the reason and substance for publishing it. Someone running a seminary may need to recall that Old Testament Survey is supposed to equip a young person to be a better pastor; it has limited significance apart from that. We should beware of plans so urgent that they keep us from knowing people.

I learned at *Step* to see interruptions as messages from my environment. I could force things to run the way I thought they should, overriding problems and objections. But if I took my eye off the clock and let interruptions actually stop me and make me think, I usually learned something about the people I worked with. Sometimes, because of what I learned, the work went ahead more smoothly. Certainly my relationships with people were better when I moved my bias for speed toward their bias for people.

The Folks Back Home
What about the pressure of expectations from our supporters?

I think first of all we need to trust them more. If we start by assuming they can never understand the real problems we face, then we will never let them be full partners in our work. We will have to always feed them encouraging stories to prop up their enthusiasm. Many of our prayer letters home are plain deceptive. They are not meant to inform but to inspire giving.

The two are not necessarily at odds. Cross-cultural ministry, with all its difficulties, is inherently interesting if you take time to explain it. People at home do grow fascinated by it, just as we did before going out. I found that the more carefully I explained our plans and problems to my supporters, the more enthusiastic they became. They knew of our frustrations, and they carried them with us. They helped us be more patient, because they supported us in the real problems we faced. They grew with us. Our support actually increased dramatically, rather than doing the usual fade-off.

But I do not think the greatest pressure really comes from our supporters. I suspect it comes from within ourselves. We imagine our supporters' disappointment because we cannot face the possibility of disappointing ourselves. We put on an image of speedy success because we cannot face the possibility of admitting failure.

For this pressure the only cure lies in the ordinary Christian life: prayer, honest fellowship, growth in the knowledge of God. Can he really contemplate us as failures? Does he truly work all things together for his pleasure? We have to pray that he will re-educate us to care not for our image of ourselves, but about him—first and last. His speed may seem excruciatingly slow, as it did for those Peter wrote to (2 Pet 3:9). But at this speed, and not American high-tech speed, he is redeeming people. We should get in step with his time.

9
True Sacrifice—
and Not-Quite-True

MY WIFE POPIE discovered the Noble-People Theorem:
When one noble person meets another, they are bound to
dislike each other.

It was discovered this way. At a particularly busy time in
our lives we were asked to take in two members of a touring
Christian drama team from America. Their accommoda-
tions had fallen through, and they had nowhere else to go.
One American group or another is always passing through
Nairobi to minister, and we were not altogether enthusiastic
about their effectiveness. But this was a case of people in need,
so we took them in. They stayed for about a week.

They were outwardly pleasant people, but by the end of
that week we were ready to throw them out the door. They
showed no interest in us, in what we were doing or even in
what we knew about Kenya. They liked to talk about their
ministry in drama—and not much else. They didn't compli-

ment our cooking; they didn't try to help with the dishes; they didn't emphasize their gratitude for hospitality. They acted, in fact, as though we ought to be grateful they had come. We felt taken for granted.

After they had gone Popie and I had a long talk about it. Why had things gone so wrong? She had the insight. She suggested that our guests had felt they were making a noble sacrifice coming to Africa. They were "important people" at home, no doubt admired for their willingness to go where God sent them—even to Africa.

And we felt noble hosting them.

They had not noticed our nobility, and we had not appreciated theirs. They were probably as irked as we, for I suppose they picked up that we were not enchanted with their contribution to Africa.

In thinking about this book I realized that the Noble-People Theorem applies to missionaries and our national hosts. When we reach our new home we think, just as the drama team did, that we have done a noble deed in just coming. A good proportion of the time, I have discovered, our hosts don't see us as noble at all. They think they are the noble ones. They welcome us in their homes. They overlook our pushiness and never mind that we have ten times the money they do. We can't recognize their nobility because it contradicts our own. The dual nobilities form a barrier between us, which I call the barrier of pride.

Gingerly Conversations

Being a missionary ought to be humbling. At home, non-Christian friends and relations are sure to think you are behaving strangely. They talk to you gingerly, as one talks to a man running for Congress under the Communist Party. Afraid you might go into a sermon, or ask for money, they skirt your career entirely. Many Christians will treat you in the same way, as someone who has gotten overenthusiastic about a cause.

Others who believe in missions will admire you. But in your new home you may not find their admiration very strengthening. They are far away. Mail is slow arriving, and a surprising number of people forget to write you, especially in the first few months when you need letters most. What admiration you can garner from these infrequent missives seems increasingly cut off from what you are doing and seeing. Your daily work is usually dogged, uncheered and unproductive. The first few times you examine a baby with malnutrition or watch teeming multitudes in the marketplace, missions seems exciting. But the glamor wears off.

Meanwhile, nobody local treats you as noble. You are just like the other missionaries, only new and ignorant. They treat you as the raw recruit. Your national hosts don't think you are noble; whatever sacrifices you have made, you still live above their level. No one can really think in his heart that you suffer by coming to live in his home. Whatever you find horrifying, he is used to.

Your best work, if done at home, would probably seem rather unsophisticated. I started a magazine in Africa and felt it was a substantial achievement. But to look at the magazine with American eyes, you would not think so. Publishing is not in an advanced state in Africa. Graphics and printing don't measure up to Western standards. Nobody in America will think me a publishing genius by looking at an issue of *Step*.

Other fields are likely to be similar. If you teach in a seminary you may deal with basic material; your knowledge of German theologians will be of little use. If you do pioneer evangelism you may see fewer converts in a year than a campus staff member makes on an American college campus in a week. Most missionary work is innovative and therefore risky and slow. Often it involves training a national leader to take over when the work is established. The hard struggle from the ground up is yours, and the glory years belong to someone else. Your whole vision may crumble when the person you trained takes his training to a better-paying job in business.

Because of the colonial past, a foreigner won't be (and probably shouldn't be) given full credit for his or her work. Nobody in his right mind would have called a public meeting of Kenyans to tell the world how wonderful I had been in starting *Step* magazine. To do so would have undermined *Step*'s success as a genuinely African publication. People let me know they appreciated my work, but privately. I got no glory.

True Humility

All this may seem calculated to teach humility. But your first reaction will probably be just the opposite. You'll feel sorry for yourself, nobly aware of the sacrifices you have made. Real humility requires that you forget these sacrifices, as though they were nothing.

This seems next to impossible. Who can sincerely echo the sentence Jesus commanded us to say, "We are only unworthy servants, who have done what was required of us"? The very words sound smarmy because we can hardly imagine them felt sincerely.

Here we touch something close to the heart of our sin and need for grace. We know that Jesus sacrificed himself "for the joy set before him." He was entirely aware of the pain and disgrace he would suffer, and he searched and prayed for another way. Yet he did not show the least evidence of showing off his self-sacrifice for others. Not at the Last Supper, not in the garden of Gethsemane, not in court, did he betray the slightest self-pity. He showed concern for the strength of his disciples under temptation. He looked ahead, to the joy he believed in but could not see.

His example ought to remind us of our calling to be like him in our smaller difficulties. We should take our sacrifices without thought of earthly glory: of applause, of fame, of admiration. We should sacrifice for the joy we will get on the other side of death, and for that only. If we have this attitude, our pride will be no barrier to those we serve. We will not then be Noble People.

But this requires a change of attitude so deep there is nothing for it but prayer. It is beyond our reach. Only God can help.

What do we pray for, though? I need something positive—a joy before me—to imagine as I pray. We know what the disease is like, but what is the medicine? It is, I believe, the kind of love you find in a family. That is what I pray for.

Memoirs written by the relatives of famous people always interest me. Their world-famous brother is not Henry Sarsky, the virtuoso pianist, but Hank who was too shy to make conversation. Matilda Bruno, the elegant *dame d'affaires,* is only Matty who was always chatting about boys. Their fame and glory are an accretion, not a primary quality, and they are treated not with awe but with fondness or annoyance or sibling envy. Count on it: if someone writes with awe about his famous brother, they must have been ten years apart.

In families there are no pretty sisters or plain sisters. Love, or lack of it, is not based on externals. It is deeper, more wholistic, not earned at all. I love my brother because he is my brother, and not because he is a fine historian. My pleasure in discovering he is an outstanding historian comes only because I already love him. It pleases me that he has value to others as well as to me. For those who know this kind of love, nothing is more valuable; and for those who lack it, no amount of glory can compensate for its absence.

I lost some glory in becoming a missionary, as all missionaries will. I did not advance in my career or my wealth. Whatever I did of value goes largely unrecognized. But I count myself supremely blessed in this: I did experience in Kenya some genuine appreciation from friends—small doses to be sure, but of such wholesome quality that those years became the greatest of my life so far. It is this appreciation that will, in massive quantities, constitute glory on the Day of Judgment. The admiration of the world, even the Christian world, will seem like froth, gone with the sun's next rising.

This is the love we can pray for. It begins here on earth with our family. It can extend to friends and working partners, even in cultures different from our own. But it comes, in the end, from God. In our prayers we can ask to receive it. But more essentially we can ask God to remold us so that this kind of love satisfies us and fills our hearts with joy, so that whatever admiration we give up just doesn't matter.

If we can imagine a person so stripped of pride, so nourished by genuine, deep appreciation that he wants nothing else, we imagine a person who has few barriers to other people, no matter what their culture. His shell is dissolved. He meets you wholly when you meet him. Jesus on earth must have been such a person. He seems to have compelled people, almost stunned them, in a manner quite beyond the power of his words or his miracles.

An Overdose of Idealism?

The question comes to me as I close this book: Have I been too idealistic? Have I pressed too hard on people who don't get beyond cultural barriers?

You might gather from these pages that an ideal missionary will move in a foreign culture as freely as a fish in the sea. Perhaps that is ideal, but we are not ideal material for it. Most of us will only partially succeed at becoming free in the culture we join.

Should we even try? Should a missionary seek complete assimilation into his new home, or should he seek simply to survive? Should he "go native," or merely do his work?

Such questions encourage an all-or-nothing mentality which only hurts us. We are not all-or-nothing people. At whatever we try, we succeed some of the time and fail some of the time.

Too great an idealism will encourage us either to despair or to become defensive about how we live. Because it makes our chief concern how we measure up to a standard, it will build the barrier of pride. Ideals are stars we navigate by. So long as we stay rooted to this earth, we should not frustrate ourselves by complaining that they remain beyond our reach.

We are what we are, by the grace of God. We fail often. But knowing what we ought to be, we do not let our failings sidetrack us. Accepting God's forgiveness means accepting ourselves as weak and sometimes willfully wrong-minded. But it also means accepting that we can be of use, superb use, in the universe.

One of my friends spent a year traveling around the world visiting missionaries, and what he saw shook his faith. He had thought of missionaries as God's choice messengers. What he saw didn't measure up to the ideal. "I had to wonder," he told me, "whether the Christian faith was nothing more than a cosmic joke." He saw the most important work in the world being mishandled by people he described as incompetents. Could God be serious?

Such overgeneralizations are sparked by shattered ideals. A good many missionaries have had similar feelings. Some, seeing the real-life failings of their mission, have packed up and gone home.

Is it a joke? Maybe it is, in line with the one Paul told: "It seems to me that God has put us apostles on display. . . . We have been made a spectacle to the whole universe. . . . We are fools for Christ. . . . We have become the scum of the earth, the refuse of the world" (1 Cor 4:9-10, 13).

I don't think Paul was purely using sarcasm. From a certain point of view his words are true. Who, beyond a few faithful, believed him more than a religious fanatic, traveling the world to visit tiny, struggling bands of followers, whose faith he had constantly to jack up or correct? Now we call him a great theologian. Then he was strictly a nobody, fixing tents to pay his keep. But God used such foolishness to change the world.

And he has used other missionaries in the same way. Making fun of missionaries is nothing new; you can find it in Thackeray. Missionaries may not, in fact, be brilliant, capable or even especially good. We may deserve fun. But God has used missionaries to spread his Word. He is still using us. He will use us. For God is always using the improbable, forever working from outside the center.

New Centers from Old Backwaters

Paul is one case in point. He had no great congregations. He didn't see thousands of converts, as Peter and the Jerusalem church did. Basic morality seemed to elude Paul's little half-pagan congregations. Surely they were not impressive compared to the booming Jerusalem church, where the Twelve taught and did miracles, where the council through the Spirit directed church policy.

But within a few decades that great Jerusalem church had disappeared. Beyond the pages of the New Testament, the only church we know is a gentile church. The small, struggling work Paul had begun spread throughout the Roman world. To be a missionary is to be an heir of Paul's mission, through which the church escaped death in Jerusalem.

Jerusalem was demolished, just as Jesus had said. For the next several centuries Rome held the power. The center of church authority and wisdom, of theological and philosophical depth, of artistic beauty, had moved to Rome. But then Rome came under military attack. Christendom was again at stake.

Who thought much about the Irish monasteries, far north in a bitter climate, little havens of learning amid unschooled pagans? As the empire stood in danger, who could doubt that Rome was where Christian leaders belonged? But when the empire fell, it was not Rome which enabled Christianity to survive. The obscure monks of Ireland, always somewhat footloose, spread the gospel throughout the continent, leaving their beloved island to establish Christian communities among the very savages who had torn Rome down. The gospel survived and spread—but not from Rome. It spread from the periphery, from the little known, from the insignificant but faithful few.

We may be in the middle of another such story. The great

Protestant missionary thrust began in the nineteenth century. (It is somewhat shocking that those following the principle of the authority of Scripture needed three hundred years after Luther to discover the Great Commission.) But even in Victorian times, not all Christians respected missionary work. Why should one worry about the souls of brown and black people? Let them alone, some said: Christianity is for Europeans and Americans. The same thing is still said, though by now the powerful indigenous churches of Asia, Africa and South America have outgrown those of Europe.

Even American Christians do not, I think, much believe that missions is the center of God's work. In America we have all the books, all the great speakers and preachers, all the new developments in ministry. Missionaries do noble work. But important? Crucial? Do people line up to hear missionaries talk when they come home? Are accounts of their work frequent best sellers?

Who knows what surprises God may have in mind? Who knows whether our great American church will last? Who knows what the world will be like in fifty years? We do know this: God is preparing a feast of praise for himself, whereby every person will kneel before him and every language harmonize in his praise. Missionaries are not the only way God works toward this, but it is plainly obvious they are at the heart of the vision, for missionaries alone are trying to awaken a people of God in every nation, every language. There is enough glory in that to make up for any we may miss on earth. If this is a joke, let us laugh with joy.

The New Community

This spread of God's kingdom is not merely mechanical, however, not simply a question of making certain that the message is proclaimed everywhere. God could do that with machines or angels. He chooses to use people so that the goal of fellowship may be contained, in seed, in the very means of getting there. The first fruits of God's kingdom, like the full harvest, must include the wild harmonization of praise in many languages and tunes.

If we are not concerned to find this fellowship across the barriers of culture, we make ourselves into gospel machines— all work and no soul. Factory workers may put together computers, yet have no idea what a computer is or how to use it. But such deadened sense is not meant for us: God isn't dragging bodies into heaven, but making persons fit for it. He will touch our lives with a current of his Spirit, which links impossible differences together: God to man, and man to man.

I hope this book has demonstrated that this linkage is not an easy one, for the barriers of our differences are not easily or commonly penetrated. Nor are these barriers bridged by some mechanical infusion of grace: God helps us to make friends of people different from ourselves only as we labor to understand, to expose ourselves to new experiences, and to wait in prayer for light to break. Grace is never divided from work: it impels us to work, to struggle, to suffer. If we shy away from this work, which is by no means all pleasure, we are equally shying from God's grace. Only as we struggle to birth the new community shall we know the full power of the resurrection, power which enables us, with all Christians, to "grasp how wide and long and high and deep is the love of Christ"—love which extends to and incorporates the most different of people.

Notes

Preface
[1]C. S. Lewis, *Reflections on the Psalms* (New York: Harcourt Brace Jovanovich, 1964), pp. 1-2.

Chapter 1: The Snake & the Egg
[1]Isak Dinesen, *Out of Africa* (New York: Vintage Trade Books, Random House, 1972), pp. 18-19.

Chapter 2: Culture Fatigue
[1]T. Wayne Dye, "Stress-Producing Factors in Cultural Adjustment," *Missiology: An International Review* (a journal; n.d.).
[2]Unless otherwise noted, quotations from missionaries are from personal correspondence.
[3]Elizabeth Brewster and Thomas Brewster, *Bonding and the Missionary Task* (Dallas, Tex.: Lingua House, 1982).
[4]"Rock of Ages."

Chapter 3: Bridging the Chasm of Culture
[1]"Good," comments one ex-missionary anthropologist. "But let's remember to [push ourselves] tranquilly (!) lest we be classed with those mad dogs and Englishmen who run about in the noonday sun, or those measurement-mad Americans."
[2]Bill McConnell, missionary to Brazil, provides a delightful discussion of cultural differences in time perception in *The Gift of Time* (Downers Grove, Ill.: InterVarsity Press, 1983)—*ed.*

Suggested Reading

Brewster, Elizabeth, and Brewster, Thomas. *Bonding and the Missionary Task.* Dallas, Tex.: Lingua House, 1982. Available from Academic Publications, Summer Institute of Linguistics, 7500 W. Camp Wisdom Rd., Dallas, TX 75236.

Hopler, Thom. *A World of Difference.* Downers Grove, Ill.: InterVarsity Press, 1981.

Kohls, L. Robert. *Survival Kit for Overseas Living.* Chicago: Intercultural Network/Systran Publications, 1979. Available from the publishers at 70 W. Hubbard St., Chicago, IL 60610.

McConnell, William T. *The Gift of Time.* Downers Grove, Ill.: InterVarsity Press, 1983.